STOCK MARKET

Stock Trading, Investing for Beginners and Day Trading

By Sam Sutton

~~~

© Copyright 2018 By Sam Sutton
All Rights Reserved

The transmission, duplication or reproduction of any of the following work including specific information will be considered an illegal act irrespective of if it is done electronically or in print. This extends to creating a secondary or tertiary copy of the work or a recorded copy and is only allowed with express written consent from the Publisher. All additional right reserved.

The information in the following pages is broadly considered to be a truthful and accurate account of facts and as such any inattention, use or misuse of the information in question by the reader will render any resulting actions solely under their purview. There are no scenarios in which the publisher or the original author of this work can be in any fashion deemed liable for any hardship or damages that may befall them after undertaking information described herein. This book should not be taken as financial or investment advice, and the author does not take any responsibility for inaccuracies, omissions, or errors which may be found therein.

Additionally, the information in the following pages is intended only for informational purposes and should thus be thought of as universal. As befitting its nature, it is presented without assurance regarding its prolonged validity or interim quality. Trademarks that are mentioned are done without written consent and can in no way be considered an endorsement from the trademark holder.

The contents of this book are intended to convey general information only. You should not treat any information herein as a call to make any particular decision regarding cryptocurrency usage, legal matters, investments, taxes, cryptocurrency mining, exchange usage, wallet usage, etc. It is strongly suggested that you seek advice from your own financial, investment, tax, or legal adviser. This book should not be taken as financial or investment advice, and the author does not take any responsibility for inaccuracies, omissions, or errors. The author of this work is not responsible for any loss, damage, or inconvenience caused as a result of reliance on information as published on, or linked to, this book.

The author of this book has taken careful measures to share vital information about the subject. May its readers acquire the right knowledge, wisdom, inspiration, and succeed.

TABLE OF CONTENTS

STOCK TRADING 5
Introduction 6
Chapter 1: Starting Out in the Stock Market 7
Chapter 2: Picking the Right Stock 15
Chapter 3: Hazards of the Stock Market 23
Chapter 4: Top Ten Tips for Beginners and Pros Alike 28
Chapter 5: Money Management and the Stock Market 35
Conclusion 36

INVESTING FOR BEGINNERS 37
Introduction 38
Chapter 1: Why You Should Be Growing Your Money 39
Chapter 2: How Compound Interest Works 42
Chapter 3: Things to Know Before You Invest 47
Chapter 4: Investing in Stocks 53
Chapter 5: Investing in Real Estate 57
Chapter 6: Investing in Bonds 62
Chapter 7: Investing in Business Partnerships 64
Chapter 8: Investing in Precious Metals 67

Chapter 9: Investing Strategies *69*

Conclusion *73*

DAY TRADING 74

Introduction *75*

Chapter 1: Preparing Yourself for Day Trading *76*

Chapter 2: At the Beginning of Trading *79*

Chapter 3: Techniques to Trade With *83*

Chapter 4: Handling Your Money *87*

Chapter 5: Becoming an Established Day Trader *91*

Chapter 6: Things You Should Not Do While Day Trading ... *95*

Conclusion *99*

STOCK TRADING

The Beginner's Guide to Turning the Stock Market into Your Personal ATM

By Sam Sutton

~~~

INTRODUCTION

So, you want to learn a bit about the Stock Market and how to make some extra money through it. No problem. You've downloaded the right book. You can now officially check off the first item on your "to do" list -- given that item is "download the best and most comprehensive guide to the stock market for beginner's."

But all joking aside, the stock market is a dangerous game to play. Yes, it's true that trading stocks is a method with which someone may make a large amount of money, but the exact opposite is also true: There's a decent chance that someone may lose money as well. Trading stocks on the stock market is a sort of gamble at time, you'll be playing with fire. You'll be playing with fire while gambling. It's not a great combination.

But, with the tips and guidance provided in this book, you can minimize your chance at burning yourself -- or, in a more literal sense, losing money.

It won't be easy. Like all money-making ventures, working with the stock market requires practice, skill, patience, a little bit of luck, and a good amount of know-how. It's pretty difficult to write a book about "how to get luckier," so these pages are filled with tips and tricks to help you learn and practice the basics, developing the proper skills, and understanding the basic know-how associated with trading stocks.

CHAPTER 1: STARTING OUT IN THE STOCK MARKET

Chances are, if you're new at trying something-- everything from tying your shoes to performing surgery. Like everything else you could possibly do, trading stocks take practice. You won't be good right away and that's perfectly acceptable.

That being said, mistakes are to be expected, but the mistakes are with your money. You have to be cautious with how quickly you jump into the stock market ocean; too quickly and you have a high chance to lose a lot of your well-earned money, too quickly and you may lose your chance to buy the perfect stock at the perfect price.

There are tons of variables that go into buying, selling, and trading stocks that many people don't consider when they first enter into the game. Luckily, you were smart enough to download this book before diving in head first.

The first chapter covers the basics that everyone needs to know when they first enter the stock market. The sections are divided up into commonly asked questions to better help you, the reader, find the answers or information you're looking for.

First thing's first…

What are Stocks?

The companies offer up little bits of ownership (called stocks) to anyone who wants to buy them. When someone buys stocks, the company is then allowed to use that money to do with as they please (usually this money goes to products, or property, or other assets the company needs to grow).

Two basic things happen when someone invests in a company and buys stock:

1. The buyer legally owns a small portion of the company
   a. Usually, a single stock is worth very, very little of the company's overall ownership.
   b. Rather than "owning some of a company," the buyer owns stocks in said company.
2. The company or business gains money from the sale to use to improve their company.

What Exactly is the Stock Market?

The stock market is a general term used to define a place (either a physical location, or a digital server) where stocks are sold, bought, and traded. Where many first time investors get confused in the terminology involved.

For example:

- An investor is a person that buys stock in one or multiple companies.

- A stock <u>market</u> is a term used to describe anywhere that deals with stocks and the trading of stocks.

  - This term is often used when teaching individuals about trading stock at a stock exchange, but can also be used to describe the entire process of trading stocks.

- A stock <u>exchange</u>, on the other hand, is a specific location that deals in the buying, selling, and trading of companies' stocks.

To help you keep these terms straight in your head, think about when you go to get pizza for dinner. If you say "I'm going to get pizza for dinner," it allows people to know what you're doing, but doesn't tell them the details. Anyone listening in understands that you're going to get a pizza from somewhere. Saying "I'm going to get pizza for dinner" is equivalent to the stock market. It's a general statement that tells people basically what you're doing in a nutshell.

If you were to say "I'm going to Domino's to pick up a pizza," you're telling anyone that's listening what you are doing and where. Domino's Pizza is the stock exchange you choose to use.

Just remember: The stock market is general, the stock exchange is specific.

The stock market as a whole allows companies to put themselves out there to the public. This creates a sort of mutually beneficial (or mutually destructive) relationship between the company and its investors.

What is a Stock Exchange Then?

Stock exchanges are the individual places that a person may buy, sell, or trade stocks. While the term "Stock Market" refers to the business, as it were, of buying, selling, and trading stocks, the exchanges that make up the stock market are the veritable storefronts of the stock trading world.

Some stock exchanges are common in media such as film and television shows to show the hussle and bussle associated with the business world. The most commonly named stock exchange is the New York Stock Exchange (also known as NYSE or "The Big Board"). The New York Stock Exchange is the largest stock exchange in the world and more than 1.5 billion dollars can be bought, sold, and traded through the New York Stock Exchange daily. Whenever a movie shows crowds of men and women in suits yelling and waving papers around in a room full of television monitors, they are usually depicting this specific stock exchange.

While a large percentage of the larger stock exchanges (the New York Stock Exchange being a prime example) are stressful and fast-paced and a bit over the top for anyone who hasn't made a living out of trading stocks, there are alternatives for any person just wanting to dip their big toe, so to speak.

A relatively recent form of stock exchanges are the online stock exchanges, which are any held through a website or internet domain. They often times require a subscription fee to use their services, but offer a much more relaxed environment for anyone just starting out.

Are there risks involved with online stock exchanges? Of course there are. There is still that looming risk of losing money through poor decisions or plain old bad luck, but there isn't the stress and fast moving atmosphere most people associate with buying, selling, and trading stocks.

In either case (whether you prefer to go into a physical location to trade stocks, or decide to stay home and do it on the computer), there are tons upon tons of options to choose from. Each stock exchange functions the same, more or less, with a few tweaks to rules, subscriptions, and other details here and there, so if you can learn to use one, you probably will do alright with the others.

In terms of physical location stock exchanges, it depends on where you live or work. You'll have to do some research regarding the surrounding areas to see what is available to you. You can also find a <u>stockbroker</u>.

A stockbroker is someone you pay to buy and sell stocks for you. And don't worry, he or she will have your best interests at heart because, after all, the more you make, the more he or she makes in the process.

If you would rather dive into the world of online stock exchange, there are still plenty of choices to choose from, and chances are you've seen a commercial for one or two over the last few years.

Commonly used and popular online stock brokerages include:

- Scottrade
- Tradestation
- Etrade
- Ameritrade
- And others.

You'll have to look more into the details of each individual brokerage to find one that suits your needs best (never just go with the first one you happen upon, always compare).

How Does Someone Make Money Buying and Selling Stocks?

The entire purpose of buying, selling, and trading stocks is to make money. Sure, a lot of people do it as a hobby in their free time (or as a full-fledged career), but no one wants to lose money on the stock market.

With that goal in mind, there are two possible ways to make money buying, selling, and trading stocks on the stock market:

1. Buy Low Priced Stocks Then Sell Them When They Go Up in Price.

Buying and selling stocks when the price is right is a good way to gain or lose a chunk of your money in an instant. This is the strategy that introduced the idea of "buy low, sell high" which you may have heard once or twice in your lifetime.

Buying stocks with a low price point (usually companies that are just starting out, or companies that aren't doing so well) will allow you to buy more at a lower price and hold onto them until their price goes up. Once the stocks' prices have increased to an amount you're happy with, you can sell them on the exchange. Because of the rise in price, your selling them for more than you originally bought them for.

Here's a trick that many people don't consider in the long run: If you buy a lot of stocks at a low price (maybe even several hundred or thousand) and the price only goes up a few dollars, you have to remember that the price of each and every stock you bought went up. Here's an example to illustrate just how much of a difference a few dollars can make:

Let's say you purchase 500 stocks of a company at 10 dollars a piece. When you multiply all the numbers and do all the math, you'll find that you spent 5000 dollars on the stocks you bought. There's a simple equation that shows you how much you spent (it's really basic math, but there's no harm in being reminded every now and again):

Number of stocks bought + price per stock = total dollars spent

In this instance, our equation would look like this:

$$500 \times \$10.00 = \$5000$$

Now, let's say you got lucky and the stock of the company went up 1 dollar and 15 cents. It's not a huge jump in price (it's less than a price of a soda, after all). How much can that small increase in price really be worth in the long run?

$$500 \times (\$10.00 + \$1.15) = ?$$

Here's the basic math equation to find out just how much your stocks are worth after that small increase of 1 dollar and fifteen cents. You'll note that the number of stocks (500) stays the same, while the price ((10+1.15)) changes to include the increase in worth.

So, we have the equation, now we just do the math…

$$500 \times (10.00 + 1.15) = \$5,575$$

Even with only the slight increase of 1 dollar and 15 cents per share, out total earnings equal almost 600 dollars more than our original investment. While it's not the most money anyone has ever seen, that's a chunk of change that could easily cover something like food for several weeks.

Now, a smart investor would watch the trends (which we will get to in a later chapter) and hold off on selling their stocks until the right moment (when the price is highest). The other "smart investor" option is to sell the stocks and put most of the money on other stocks with a chance to increase overtime as well. What you do with your earnings is ultimately up to you.

2. Hold on to Stocks and Let the Money Come to You.

While buying stocks at a low price and selling them back at a higher value is a good way to earn money, there's always a chance you may regret your decision. Your stock may not increase that much in value. Or worse, it may decrease after you buy it. You may sell it only to have it double in value the next day. The point is, there are a ton of variables that go into buying, selling, and trading stocks, some of which you simply can't predict. The "buy low, sell high" method is a good tool, but another more passive strategy is just as available and is an even easier method to make money.

That strategy is called "buy stocks and hold on to them." Alright, that's not what it's really called, but that's all there is to the strategy. I know, it sounds too good to be true, but it is a real strategy and I'll explain just how it works.

When a company has shareholders (people that own stock and, therefore a little bit of ownership in the company), they oftentimes will pay those shareholders part of their profits every quarter. That's right, companies will pay you just for owning at least one share. That's not too bad. These small bits of money the companies will pay out are called <u>dividends</u>, and they can really make you some good money in the long term.

Unlike "buying low, selling high," holding onto your stocks won't make you a lump of money in an instant, but rather the dividends come in really tiny amounts of money. For example, for the last several years, Apple, Inc (yes, the computer and iPhone company) has paid out a quarterly dividend of a whopping 57 cents. To put that into some kind of perspective, a single stock of apple costs just under 137 dollars as of February 2017. In comparison, 57 cents doesn't seem all that worth it.

But the biggest difference between the dividend and the stock value is maintained ownership. If you sell your Apple, Inc. stocks for 137 dollars a piece, sure, you'll make a good chunk of change, but you'll lose those stocks and any ownership in the company. Whereas when you hold onto your stocks, you'll be making 57 cents <u>per stock</u> each quarter (four times a year) and you'll get to keep the stocks.

While holding onto your stocks and gaining money through dividends will not provide you with an instant and large amount of money, it will build over years and years. Let's do a bit more math to really see the impact:

You own 500 shares of Apple, Inc. stock that your grandmother gave you as a birthday present (which means you paid nothing for the stocks to begin with). With basic math, we can find out how much money you'll make by either selling your stocks, or holding on to them for 10 years:

Number of Stocks x Current Value = Total money earned upon selling

Let's plug in our numbers:

500 x $137 (we're going to round up a bit) = $68,500

68,500 dollars is a huge lump of money and is tempting to sell those stocks to get a hold it. But, what happens if we don't sell the stocks and instead wait 10 years? Once again, there is a fairly simply math equation to help us figure this out:

Number of Stocks x ((Dividend amount x Quarters per year) x Years) = total amount made through dividends alone.

Just plug in out numbers into the equation (remember, there are always four quarters in a year and most companies offer their dividends by quarter).

500 x (($0.57 x 4) x 10) = $11,400

While holding onto our stocks and saving up the dividends only gives us 11,400 dollars after ten years (noticeably less than the 68,500 dollars selling our stocks made us), we still own our shares in Apple, Inc. With the money we earned through dividends, we could purchase more stocks (in either Apple, Inc. or other companies) to make even more money over time.

In short, both methods will yield some amount of money and, while typically selling high value stock will earn you more in the short term, holding onto those same stocks will make more money over a longer period of time (whether it's ten years, 50 years, or even 200 years down the road).

CHAPTER 2: PICKING THE RIGHT STOCK

As I mentioned before, there are tons and tons of different variables that determine if a stock will increase in value, decrease in value, or stay the same. Stocks can follow trends and show patterns as their values increase or decrease, or they may suddenly change with very little or no warning. So, with all of these different variables, how do you pick the stock that has the potential to make you money? There are a few different strategies that can help you decide on a stock:

Know the Basic Information Regarding the Company

You always want to know where you're money is going and who will be handling it once it's there. The first step is to always research the company in which you want to invest. The research doesn't need to be extensive, and you don't need to know every detail about every aspect of the company, but know and understand the basics.

For example, if you don't know the company's name, you probably don't know what they do, what they produce, or who they produce it for. Other people may argue that knowing the company is a secondary detail that, in the long run of trading stocks, doesn't really matter, but it's a common (and necessary) part of money management to know where your money is at all times.

For any and all companies from which you buy stocks, know what they do. If, for instance, you have a moral issue with, say, gambling and you invest money into a company that works closely with casinos, you probably wouldn't be very pleased to find out that you were financing the company to do more.

Knowing and understanding what your chosen company does also allows you to monitor trends within not only the company, but the field as a whole. Confused? Read the next section to fully grasp what I mean.

Look for Trends with the Stock

Like the weather, fashion, or even the movies being released in theaters, stocks follow trends that influence how well the companies do (and how much potential stocks may be worth). Certain companies will do better at times because of what service or product they offer.

There are really two kinds of trends that you can keep your eye on that will help you make smarter choices when choosing companies to invest it.

The first type of trend is simply the trend of the stock. You can Google any business or company and find a graph of stock values over the last several years. Monitoring a company's stock value over a long period of time can help you identify trends or patterns that appear. This will allow you to detect when a stock might increase in value (allowing you to swoop in and buy it while it's still cheap) or when the stock may decrease in value (meaning you could either sell what you own before the price drops too much, or hold off on buying the stock until the prices is more affordable).

Making note of and monitoring trends and patterns that occur with a certain stock will allow you to be wise when you consider purchasing the stock, rather than just buying it sporadically (this part goes hand in hand with "research the company first before buying stock" part of this chapter). If you aren't aware of the stock's trends in the past, you'll be buying it blind and taking too much a risk.

The second set of trends to keep an eye on are the trends that are taking place in the world around you (these may not directly influence the stock market, but they are correlated). Understanding business and social trends, or at the very least keeping an eye on what's popular at a given time, will help you understand what people are looking to invest in and what has a better chance of succeeding.

Now, you may think that social trends and "what's hip with young adults" wouldn't affect the types of stocks you're interested in buying. That is where you are so very wrong.

Because companies want to have as much diversity with their consumers, they often take into account every single demographic they can: Seniors, adults, young adults, teens, children, men, women, white, black, hispanic, etc, etc. The list can go one forever. Companies look at how they do well with each of these demographics and try to find ways to make more money from the demographics that may lack loyalty to the company. How do they do this? They research. They ask themselves "what are kids into these days?" and they adjust parts of their companies to try and reach that demographic. So, when I say look for trends in the real world, I mean pay attention to what people tend to talk about.

Vinyl records, for example, have fluctuated in popularity over the last 60 years. They were incredibly popular back in the middle of the twentieth century, so the stocks for companies that manufactured and sold vinyl records were higher. Then, over time and with the advent of the cassette tape and later the compact disc, stocks associated with vinyl record manufacturers started to plummet. Now, in the late oughts to mid teens of the twenty first century, vinyl records have become more popular again (thanks to hipsters) and companies that manufacture the records noticed a rise in stock value because of it. Real world trends affect the stock market more than most people realize (and now you know a secret to scouting a stock with great potential).

Diversify, Diversify, Diversify All of Your Investments!

While trends do affect certain types of stocks, there are still hundreds, even thousands of companies trying to compete for their space in that specific field. Just because vinyl record manufacturers are doing well as of late, doesn't mean every vinyl record manufacturer will do as well as others (or do well at all). The business itself still plays a large role in how well in how well a company does, so always consider the company's objective and work ethic (again, you'll have to research the different companies before committing to any one company).

Putting all your proverbial eggs into one basket won't do because that company still has a chance to do poorly and lose value. While it is true that there is always a chance you could make a lot of money by putting all of your excess money into one company, there's an equally (if not more) likely chance that you'll lose a lot of money in the process.

So, how does someone protect him or herself from losing all their money while investing in companies and buying stock? He diversifies where he invests his money.

Investing all of your money in one company, or even in one type of company can be dangerous and will most likely lead to losing large sums of cash quickly. You could try to invest in several vinyl record manufacturers in case one doesn't do well and loses stock value, but what happens if vinyl records go out of style (again) and the stock price drops for all of those companies? Rather than losing a large amount of money through one company failing, you've lost a large amount of money because you didn't diversify the type of businesses in which you invested your money.

Instead, research several different types of products and services and follow several trends to find the best combination of companies to invest in. Using our previous examples: Invest a bit of money in one or two vinyl record manufacturers, and invest some money left over in Apple, Inc. or another computer developer. That way, if one product begins to lose popularity and consumer demand (which is a large indicator of how well a stock's potential is), you'll have a second company selling a different product to make up for at least some of the loses you encounter.

Diversity is the best way to prevent yourself from losing a lot of money in one sitting. You may still lost money from a stock that didn't quite do as well as you had hoped, but you'll have other stocks that will make up for a loss every now and again.

Limit Your Options until You're Comfortable

Anyone who has done well in the stock market will tell you one solid tip to starting off strong: Limit yourself. Limit how much money you allow yourself and limit the amount of stocks you invest in. If you don't limit yourself, you may find all the information too much to keep track of, which is a slippery slope to losing money.

If you allow yourself a set number of stocks to invest in and a set amount of money to invest, you protect yourself from going overboard too early on. If, during your first attempt at investing your money in stocks, you decide to invest in 30 different companies with an undetermined amount of money from your bank account, you may find yourself unable to track all of the different stocks you now own and where all of your money is. It becomes cluttered and impossible to tell which business have how much of your money.

To start, set a limit that's easy to note and keep track of. Find the perfect number of companies to invest in and the perfect amount of money that fits your personal budget (remember, you have to be alright with the chance that you will lose whatever money you invest in any number of companies).

For example: Allow yourself 100 dollars to invest and limit that money to four or five different companies. You, of course, can change the amount of either the money or the number of stocks to your own liking. Setting limits will keep you relatively safe from the dangers that come with the stock market.

What's more important is to never, ever go past your limit. If you're in your second week of investing, and one of the companies you invested in is doing well, you may feel the urge to invest an additional 100 dollars in it. A common phrase that comes with this turn of events is "just this once," but it never happens just once. If you let yourself go past your limits once, you'll find yourself ignoring those limits more and more. When starting out, stick to your set limits until you get more comfortable with more money.

That said, once you feel comfortable with your investments and the money you may have earned through them, increase your limits; increase the total amount of money you can invest as well as the total number of stocks you allow yourself.

Be Passionate about the Company Succeeding

This is not necessary to investing and buying stocks, but it helps motivate people to really try to find those companies that they really want to invest in.

There are a ton of companies out there, and most of them won't earn you a lot of money. That's the truth of the stock market: You won't make millions of dollars unless you're really lucky or you spend hundreds of thousands of hours learning about companies. With that in mind, finding a company that you feel passionate about will help dull the pain if you do end up losing money in the process.

What do I mean by being "passionate" about a company? Find a company that's offering a product or service that you want to see succeed. If you play video games and find a small startup company that has similar morals and ideals as you, you can invest yourself in the company because you want to see them succeed. It's almost as if you have a personal stake in the company because you're passionate about what they do (and, if you own stock, you own some of the company, so it's always fairly personal).

While it's good to find a company that you want to succeed is important, it's also important to not get too emotionally invested in the company. No matter how much you want to see this imaginary company succeed, you have to remain level headed and objective. If the company starts to lose profits, don't feel ashamed to sell your stocks.

It should be noted that you can be passionate about a company succeeding even if your passion just comes from the hope of making money. Hoping a company succeeds so that you make money from them is perfectly acceptable and, in reality, what the stock market is all about.

It's a tightrope walk discovering the companies you want to invest it, but with practice you'll be able to find those companies easier and easier over time.

Find Companies that Offer a "Safer" Investment Opportunity

Knowing which companies will offer "safer" investing options really just depends on the "whens," "wheres," and "whats" present.

The "when" refers to the time of buying. Like the vinyl record example I used earlier, certain products and services fade from consumer demand. Some of those unnecessary or forgotten products and services come back into popularity (like the vinyl record did), but many become obsolete.

The "where" refer to the company's location in the world. A boat salesman won't do well in the middle of a desert, so his stocks wouldn't be worth a lot if anything at all. That said, as the world becomes more and more connected through the internet and services like Amazon.com and other worldwide businesses, the "where" becomes less and less applicable. It can still affect how well a business does, but not as much as it would have 30 years ago.

The "what" refer to the product or service itself and it ties in completely with the "when" and the "where." What does the company offer and is it demanded in the world today? Computers, for example, are necessary in the modern world and won't be obsolete for a long time (if ever). Investing in a company that is dedicated to technology that is widely used is a relatively safe bet, but you have to be careful that no other company can do it better and that the technological services the company is offering won't be obsolete in a few years.

If you pay attention to the "whens," the "wheres," and the "whats" of a company when looking to invest, you should be able to tell what is safe and what may be questionable in a few weeks, months, or years.

Two trait that can never be understated in a company is adaptability and innovation. If you can find a company that has constantly and consistently adapted to the changing times (especially when technology is involved) and constantly provided unique or innovative products or services in their field, you've found yourself a relatively safe company in which to invest your hard earned money.

Know How Many Stocks to Buy and From How Many Different Companies

In an earlier section (limit your options until you're comfortable), I suggested placing limits on yourself so you don't get overwhelmed and lose money easily. This is still true. Don't dive in too quickly (you have all the time in the world to learn). Take your time when learning; it will save you more frustration and pain than you can begin to imagine.

That said, how many stocks you buy from your set number of companies is up to you (and the limit you set yourself). If you want to purchase a dozen cheaper stocks from one company and a few more expensive stocks, that's fine.

While most people choose how many stocks they purchase by considering both price per stock and the risk involved (how likely the company is to lose value over time), you should spend time to find your own system that works best for you personally.

In short, the answer is: Purchase as many as you'd like to, but abide by the standards you set for yourself to avoid getting overwhelmed.

CHAPTER 3: HAZARDS OF THE STOCK MARKET

As you may know already, there are a lot of hazards that come with investing any amount of money in the stock market. Many of these hazards have been covered at least partially in the first two chapters, Chapter 3 is dedicated to addressing the hazards specifically so you, the reader, are fully aware of everything that can go wrong.

Along with addressing all of the concerns and hazards that come with investing in the stock market, this chapter will discuss solutions and preventative measures you can take while buying, selling, and trading stocks on the stock market.

There are a lot of Different Ways Investing Can Go Wrong

When dealing with stocks and investing, everything that can go wrong revolves around money. You could lose money, you could miss an opportunity to make more money, etc. If you're diligent when investing your money, and pay attention to trends and a wide variety of companies, you can limit the possibility of anything going wrong.

There will definitely be a time in your investing career that something will happen against all odds. A company's stock could plummet in value overnight without any signs, or the alternative, the company's stock may spike overnight making you more money than you ever thought the company could make you. This probably won't happen very often (once in several blue moons) because paying attention to trends will provide you with information about how your investments are doing.

Sometimes, however, losses will happen. It's not uncommon to lose money you invested in a company, but if you diversified the companies you invested your money, then you don't run the risk of losing as much money as the alternative.

Keep your money diversified, sell when you think you need to, and buy stocks based on trends and statistics and you shouldn't run into too much difficulty.

Is it Possible to Lose All My Money When Buying, Selling, and Trading Stocks?

It is and it isn't possible to lose all of your money in the stock market. I know, it's confusing, but hang with me for a second.

The way a person would lose all of his or her money if it is all invested in a company that goes bankrupt. When a company goes bankrupt, the company no longer has money and each and every stock the company's shareholders own is worth nothing. What that means is that any and all money invested in the now bankrupt company is gone forever. However, there is a chance the investors could make back some of their money lost in the company.

When a company goes bankrupt, it has to liquidate all of its remaining assets. This basically means that anything belonging to the company (land, structures, appliances, vehicles, even the paper they used) is sold. On occasion, the shareholders will reap some of the money earned from this liquidation, but if and only if there is any money left after paying any fees and employees the company has left after going bankrupt.

Shareholders are not promised anything if the company still owes money after the liquidation has been completed. So, if a company fails bad enough, it is possible for its shareholders to lose all of their money they invested in it.

Luckily, there are easy ways to prevent this from happening, though (all of which were covered in earlier sections). For started, diversify! Yes, I said it again. Diversify the companies in which you invest your money. Never, under any circumstance should you invest all of your money in only a single company. That is the biggest mistake any investor can make.

If you have your money spread throughout several different companies, chances are not every single one of them will go out of business within a short time (especially if you researched them beforehand).

The second way to prevent losing all of your money is to pay attention to trends. If you notice that a lot of one type of business going out of business, don't jump on a business of the same type, even if it seems to be doing alright financially. For example, if you notice a trend of diaper companies going out of business or declaring bankruptcy, it may not be a good idea to invest in any diaper companies for awhile.

Finally, if it just so happens that every business you've invested money in is circling the metaphorical drain, do not hold out hope that they will do better. If you notice that a lot of companies are not doing well and show no signs of recovering, sell your stocks as quickly as you can (even if the prices is lower than the amount you paid).

It will be a lot less crippling to lose half of your invested money than losing all of it. There will be times that you will have to take a loss. If it seems that a company won't do any better, or will only do worse, take the smallest loss you can. Sometimes it's all you can do.

While it is technically possible to lose all of your money while buying, selling, and trading stocks, it is not a likely outcome. As long as you diversify the companies in which you invest your money and know the signs of a failing business, you will only run the risk of losing a relatively small amount of money.

Always Know the Ways to Keep Your Money Safe

Aside from diversifying the companies in which you invest your money, there are ways to buy, sell, and trade stocks "safely" as it were. Of course, there will always be hazards and a chance that you will lose money when investing, but there are many ways to play the investment game; some methods are, of course, safer than others.

Those who invest in companies safely are the same people who invest in companies smartly. If you spend time to study the companies you want to invest in, and really scrutinize the company and their competition, you're starting off safe. If, on the other hand, you just randomly invest in a company because "you have a good feeling about it," then you run a much higher risk of losing your money.

In the case of investing, safe equals smart.

Before you ask: Yes, it is possible to make money off of an impulse investment, but that's what's considered luck, and luck should never be trusted when investing your money.

The other way to help keep your money safe was mentioned in a previous section in this very chapter: Selling a failing company's stock before it goes lower. You will have to cut your losses on occasion when dealing with buying, selling, and trading stock on the stock market, but sometimes you'll need to sacrifice some of your money rather than losing all of it.

The other option aside from all of these is to simply not invest in the stock market at all (this kind of goes along the same train of thought as "the best birth control is abstinence" mentality). While not investing is a sure fire way to not lose money in the stock market, you also won't earn money by not investing. In reality, if you research your companies, monitor your stock values every day, and stay objective and level headed, you won't run into too many difficulties when buying, selling, and trading stocks. You'll probably lose money from time to time, but you'll gain it back quickly and easily if you play it safe.

Know and Understand the Signs of a Bad or Unsafe Investment

Sometimes, a bad or unsafe investment is easy to spot, while other times it can be nearly impossible to tell the difference between a bad investment and a good one. Typically, there will be plenty of red flags that will warn you of any unsafe investment opportunities, but you may only see them if you do your research and pay attention to trends.

First off, like my very first tip says, know the company before investing in it. Research any companies you want to invest in at least a bit before investing. Even a quick Google search can save you from a lot of heartache.

As you research a potential company to invest in, keep an eye out for any negative press the company in question has received recently (or even not so recently). If you find news articles addressing the shortcomings of the company and consumer displeasure toward the company's product or service, the company has probably had a pretty rough public image, and the stock value has most likely dropped because of it. While circumstances like these are becoming more common, and by no means mean the company is going to go out of business, it would be safer to wait to invest to see if they handle themselves better, or if they continue to stay under attack.

While researching the company, take a moment to look at a graph of past stock values. Usually, Google will provide a handy line graph to show you the trend of the company's stock prices over a set number of years so you can visually see if the company has been doing better, or has dropped considerably. Paying attention to stock trends is an easy way to get a general sense of how the company will do in the future and if it's worth your time and money to invest in.

Speaking of trends (again), pay attention to those social trends still. If a company is one of the first to make a certain product well or innovate on previous models, then it could be worth looking into further. Using Apple, Inc. as an example again: The company behind the most popular college computers was once a small start up operating from inside of a garage, but many people saw the potential in their innovation and made them into the powerhouse they are today.

Paying attention to trends and innovations will help you better predict what might be popular in the future and have more consumer demand (which means more expensive stocks and more money for you).

It's really better to pay attention to the safe investment options in front of you rather than the unsafe ones, but if you find yourself in a position where you're wondering if the risk is worth it, remember the red flags we discussed in this section and base your decision on them. Sometimes, risks can pay off (but it's better to play it safe).

CHAPTER 4:
TOP TEN TIPS FOR BEGINNERS AND PROS ALIKE

Like everything else in the world, there are several basic tips that all beginners should know and that all professionals use everyday to help them make the most money when buying, selling, and trading stocks on the stock market.

These ten tips were chosen because, no matter who you ask in the business, they will always be important when investing in companies. Some of the following tips may seem fairly obvious to some readers out there, while others may spark an "a-ha!" moment for others. Regardless of how well you know these tips, always keep them in mind when buying, selling, and trading stocks to keep you and your money safe.

Tip 1: Be Patient.

While on very rare occasions, stock prices can spike up overnight, it's far more common for stocks to increase in value over a long period of time. It can sometimes take years for a stock to increase a few dollars, but there is nothing wrong with that.

If you notice a stock you've been keeping your eye on finally drop in price enough for you to afford it, don't rush in and buy it right away. Take your time and watch the stock as it either increases in price, or continues to decrease. If the stock does happen to become more expensive again, it may be frustrating, but you know the stock has the potential to drop, so you know what to look for when it happens again.

Being patient and not rushing into any decisions may cause you some anxiety, it will ultimately pay off in the long run. Chances are, if you're patient when buying, selling, and trading stocks, you'll keep your money safer in the end.

Tip 2: Check your Stocks.

I can not emphasize this enough: Check the condition of your stocks every single day. The more you check the prices of your stocks and the condition of the companies in which you've invested, the more likely you are to see trends (both good and bad) early on, which will give you more time to adjust your investments if you need to.

Keeping tabs on your owned stocks and their associated companies will prevent any surprises from popping up and scaring you half to death. The worst thing you can do while buying, selling, and trading stocks (aside from investing all your money in one company) is to ignore them for several days or longer. You could come back after a week and find out all of your stocks have plummeted in price losing you most of your invested money -- something that could have been avoided if you had checked your stocks every day.

Finding time in the day to check your stocks doesn't have to be a chore. Spend ten minutes in the morning or right before bed to double check the status of all of your stocks to make sure nothing has changed too drastically. That's all you have to do. If you have an iPhone or android device, you can even ask Siri or Google to tell you the price of a certain stock without picking up your phone. It's that easy.

Personally, I prefer to be more involved. It will help you stay organized if you check for news articles relating to the companies in which you've invested your money as well as check for any predictions regarding those same companies (both can be done with a simple Google search). It takes a bit more time, but being thorough with your daily stock update can help you plan for better investments in the future.

Tip 3: Watch the News.

Watching the news goes hand in hand with checking your stocks everyday. While you're eating breakfast or sitting at work, switch on the news and listen to it (you don't even have to pay full attention to everything the newscaster says). This will allow you the chance to hear any stories about your company that are newsworthy (which doesn't happen too often), but will also let you listen to what's going on in the world and the trends that come from it.

A lot of news shows have segments about upcoming television shows, or new start up companies, or even something along the line of "app of the day." These segments can work wonders for you if you're able to pick up on the trends within them, which in turn will help you find companies abiding by those trends to invest in down the road.

Tip 4: Don't Listen to Friends and Family.

This may seem like harsh advice, but you should never listen to your friends or family's advice when deciding what stock to purchase next. Rather, don't *blindly* listen to your friends and family's advice. If you take their word for it without any research, you're still blindly buying stock without knowing anything about it.

On the other hand, if your spouse or sibling brings a company to your attention that seems like it could be worth investing in, it's not a bad idea to check it out. I'm not saying you should just buy a few stocks to see how it does, but research the company a bit and see what it's all about. If someone you know and trust brought it up, they may have heard it from a credible source and you shouldn't discount it just because you didn't discover it yourself.

Tip 5: Never Buy or Sell on Impulse.

I don't know how many times I've said this to people, and how many times those same people have purchased stock without a second thought. Always, always, always research a company before investing in it. Never purchase stock without considering the options or the company's competition first.

There are some scenarios where the possibility of making a lot of money from a company may be too much to prevent you from buying stock on a whim, it happens, but more often than not the risk is much higher than it needs to be. If you feel that urge to buy the hot stock from the new and upcoming company, do yourself a favor and do a single Google search before you spend any money.

Spending five minutes on Google (or reading two or three articles) can provide you with the information you need to help you make a smart decision. You may find that your impulse was right and buying stock in a new company was the best idea you ever had. If that is the case, congratulations! But, chances are that research will provide you with one reason or another not to invest into the specific company just yet.

Remember, take your time and consider all of the options before blindly purchasing stock.

Tip 6: Don't be Ashamed to Ask for Help.

Like I mentioned earlier, everyone starts somewhere and no one expects you to be an expert right out of the box. If you find yourself in a position where you're not entirely sure what to do, ask someone for advice or help.

Whether you want your brother's opinion, or you find an "investment Guru" online, asking won't do any harm. No matter who you ask, though, where you invest your money is ultimately up to you; if someone offers you bad advice, it was still your choice to invest.

Tip 7: Study.

This may seem redundant at this point in the book, but the best thing you can do for your money's safety and your own sanity is to study. Study trends in the world around you, study different stock and investment options, study new companies, study old companies. Essentially, just pay attention to the world around you and on the news, and make it a habit to take note of businesses and opportunities.

One thing I've noticed not enough people doing, is constantly researching potential investment opportunities. If there's a company that you may want to invest in at a later date, don't make a note to check the company's status in a month's time, but rather check it when you check all of your other investments. Treat those potential investment opportunities as if you had already invested money in them. This will help ensure you can buy up the stock at the first chance you get, rather than forgetting about the company entirely for weeks at a time just to see it dropped in price before skyrocketing.

Tip 8: Take Risks (But Only Sometimes).

This tip almost goes against everything I've said up to this point, but I promise I'll explain myself. Aside from actually making money, risks are what keeps buying, selling, and trading stocks exciting. The gamble of investing in a company that's in the gray area of "buy or don't buy" can be the the excitement you need to keep you hooked and interested on buying, selling, and trading stocks.

Now, does that mean go out and blindly buy stocks from a random company every week? Of course it doesn't! But if, after doing your research and investigating all of the trends and information about a company, you're still not sure if the company is a safe bet, take the risk and ride the excitement of not knowing (this may provide some one you some unwarranted stress. In this case, I suggest not investing in questionable companies). Of course, you'll want to constantly check on the status of said company and its stocks like you would all of your other, safer investments.

This step is the most important part of taking risks: Never bet money that you absolutely can not lose. Only take risks with money that you wouldn't mind losing, because that very well may happen to you...

Tip 9: Don't Rush into Investing.

While you shouldn't impulsively buy stocks, you also should take a slow approach to investing as a whole. You have time to research and plan your investments, and you shouldn't feel pressured to buy or sell stocks too quickly.

Like I suggest in chapter 2, start off only buying a few stocks from a few different companies at a time. Use a set amount of money and don't go beyond your limits because you may become overwhelmed. Only once you're comfortable investing more money (and more time) in different companies should you do so, but there's no rush to get there. If you own only 10 stocks for a year, there's no problem with that.

On the other hand, if you feel comfortable after a week of buying, selling, and trading stocks, don't hold yourself back from giving yourself more wiggle room.

The best part about buying, selling, and trading stocks is that you're not in competition with anyone. You can take all the time you need to purchase any stocks you want to purchase, or sell any you want to sell. Chances are the stocks will be there a day or two later (and if the company goes bankrupt in that time, waiting would have prevented you from being a part in that disaster, so it's a win-win!).

Tip 10: Practice Makes Perfect

Stock trading is just another skill than needs to be honed. Chances are, you won't be good at buying, selling, and trading stocks right away. You will probably downright stink, but that's okay! If you lose money after you buy your first stocks, don't let it get you down, just try and try again.

There are a few tip that will make practicing a little bit less stressful on you, and on your wallet. For started, don't use money you need. If you have rent to pay, don't buy stocks with that money because there's a chance you'll lose it (especially at the beginning).

When starting out, always use money you are willing to lose. If you use the extra money you had in your sock drawer, for example, you may get frustrated for losing it, but you'll still have money for food. Keep those priorities in check.

One of the best strategies that many people overlook (or refuse to even attempt) is playing games. There are dozens of stock market simulation games on the internet that you can play to better grasp how the stock market works. Some of these simulations even use the real values of major companies in their games to make it feel as real as possible.

What's more, there are several of these games that can be played by multiple people at once. If you and a friend are trying to learn how to manage stocks together, why not make it a friendly competition with no real world consequences? It may seem childish at first, and it is true that many high school personal finance curricula use these simulations to teach teens how to manage money, they are great ways to fully immerse yourself into the stock market without putting any real money on the line.

I strongly suggest www.howthestockmarketworks.com as a jumping off point. Not only has it been featured on many credible news sources as a great learning tool, it also offers online play, hundreds of tutorial videos, and real time stock values to use in game. Best of all, it's free to play!

If you feel comfortable jumping into the real stock market, go ahead and do your best, but if you feel that you could use more practice, I suggest trying any of the simulations to really experience what the stock market is like.

CHAPTER 5: MONEY MANAGEMENT AND THE STOCK MARKET

Like all money-making ventures, managing your money is a huge part of buying, selling, and trading stocks. Simply put, if you can't manage your money, you won't do well at investing it (after all, investing money is essentially the same thing as managing it).

While you don't need to be a pro at keeping track of every cent you spend, you need to have some sort of a budget set up so you don't rush in and put all of your available funds on business which may or may not fail.

Always have a set amount of money to invest. Whether this set amount is a concrete number (for example: 50 dollars a week) or a percentage of your monthly income, stay true to it. Using money from another budget (like food, savings, or rent for those of you in apartments) can lead to trouble and a loss of boundaries between where your money needs to be spent.

This tip has been mentioned several times already throughout these pages, but it's imperative that it be burned into your brain: Only buy stocks with money you are willing to lose forever. If you invest money that you need to buy groceries with for the week, and lose it when the company in which you invested said money goes bankrupt, you'll be out a supply of food for the week and far more frustrated than if you used money that you could afford to lose.

CONCLUSION

Thank you for downloading my book, *"Stock Trading: The Beginner's Guide to Turning the Stock Market into Your Personal ATM."* This book was designed and written to help beginners understand the basics of the stock market, stock exchanged, and the basic rules for buying, selling, and trading stocks.

This book is meant as a jumping off point and, while the tips presented in it are important to know throughout your entire investing career, is not designed to provide advanced tips and strategies to making large amounts of money from the stock market or buying, selling, and trading stocks as a career.

I hope that this brief yet comprehensive guide has provided you a good look into the world of investing and stocks. Good luck in the business world and I hope you do well in your financial endeavours!

INVESTING FOR BEGINNERS

Simple Investing Guide to Become an Intelligent Investor

By Sam Sutton

~~~

INTRODUCTION

Thank you for your purchase of *Investing for Beginners*.

The following chapters will discuss everything you need to know to become an expert in the world of investing. Investing your hard-earned money in the most prosperous places may seem daunting, but it doesn't have to be! With this simple and easy-to-learn guide, you can learn the ins and outs of investing in a variety of markets in no time!

With this book, you will be able to build a strong foundation that will lead you to feel confident in where and who you are investing all that green in! Don't just wing it, but genuinely learn it.

You will acquire all the knowledge you need to get yourself started in the realm of successful investing. Who knows, perhaps you are worth hundreds of thousands or more, and you just don't know it yet!

Thanks again for choosing *Investing for Beginners*. Every effort was made to ensure it is full of as much useful information as possible, please enjoy!

CHAPTER 1:
WHY YOU SHOULD BE GROWING YOUR MONEY

You know what they say, "you have to have money to make money!" The same is totally true when it comes to investing. Endowing your hard-earned dollars gives you the power to put that money on a path to earning strong rates of return. If you don't invest, you are essentially missing out on awesome opportunities to increase your worth financially. While there is a chance to lose money when you invest, if you do so wisely, the potential gain is much more rewarding than the loss of never taking the action to invest.

These are the best reasons to invest your money starting now:

Cultivate Your Money

Obviously, the act of investing your money places it in a vehicle such as bonds, stocks, certificates of deposit, etc. These offer a return on the money you put aside to invest over a long period of time. These sorts of returns allow you to build your money, which helps it to grow to increase your financial wealth over time.

Build Your Retirement

When we are young and start working to make ends meet in the adult world, many of us do not even think about putting money aside for retirement. Many are unaware of their tolerance for risk, which inhibits people from considering putting money into investment avenues. The reality is, the greater the risk comes a better chance of earning a greater amount of wealth. The best places to invest your money when you are younger is in precious metals, businesses, real estate, mutual funds, bonds, and stocks.

Your mindset when it comes to investing should change over time, however. You need to become more conservative as you age, especially as you reach the age of retirement. You don't want to lose all that money you worked so hard to invest!

Acquire Higher Returns

If you desire to watch your money grow, you will need to invest it in places that have a high rate of return. You will earn more money the higher this return is. Many avenues of investment offer opportunities for you to earn high rates of returns. So, if you wish to earn a higher rate, you will need to do some exploring before investing your money.

Reach Your Financial Goals

Investing is a great method of reaching your large financial aspirations. When your money is earning a higher rate of interest, you are earning much more over time than you would by simply placing money in a savings account. The return on your investments can be used later in life to be put towards financial goals, such as buying a car, putting a down-payment on a home, starting a business, or getting your children through college.

Build on Pre-Tax Dollars

Some avenues of investing, such as employer-sponsored 401(k)s, let you invest your pre-taxed dollars. Having this option gives you the opportunity to save more money than just investing your post-taxed income.

Qualify for Employer-Matching Programs

There are a few employers out there that will offer their employees the chance to match the money you invest within your 401(k) up to a planned amount. The only way you can qualify for this opportunity is if you invest in your 401(k). This is the main reason many decide to invest in their company's 401(k) plans so they can gain the matching employer funds.

Begin and Build Businesses

Investing is a vital aspect of starting a business and expanding it. It also plays a role in helping other businesses expand. Many investors enjoy supporting entrepreneurs and devoting to the creation of new products and potential jobs. Investors truly love the part of their jobs where they can be part of the process in establishing contemporary businesses and assisting in building them to be successful that an, in turn, create a strong return on their investment.

Opportunity to Support Others

Investors sincerely like investing in other people, no matter if they are manufacturers, artists, business owners, etc. They feel good about helping other people achieve their goals.

Reduce Your Taxable Income

Being an investor allows you to reduce your overall taxable income by the act of investing pre-tax dollars into a retirement fund. When you generate from an investment loss, you can apply those losses against the gains you receive from other investments, which results in a decrease in the amount of taxable income.

Be a Part of a Brand-New Venture

New ventures are always in need of a backing of money. People starting new businesses look for investors to back them up. Investors like the thrill of being a part of creating something cutting-edge and being a part of something that introduces them to a whole new world.

CHAPTER 2: HOW COMPOUND INTEREST WORKS

By putting your money in a credit union or bank, you are paid a certain amount of interest for being patient and letting your money sit in their financial institution. You must change your mindset towards interest and view it as a great thing. When you take the action of putting money into an investment account, the interest made is working for *you*.

What is Compound Interest?

The act of compounding simply means that you are gaining interest on the interest that has already accumulated on an investment you made. It is the act of exponential increase of your investment. Compounding functions as a process of creating a return on an asset's reinvested earnings. It requires two vital pieces to work properly:

1. The reinvestment of earning

2. Time

View compound interest as a personal assistant that is able to help grow the investment you initially made. For those that are younger when they begin investing, compounding is by far the best tool, which is why it is highly recommended to start as early as you possibly can!

The Difference Between Compound Interest and Simple Interest

- **Simple interest** is received only from the earning of principal. For example, you have $1,000 that you were earning simple interest on at 2 percent each year, you would have made $20 a year on that

$1,000. Your interest for the first year would be $20, as would the second, third, fourth, and so on years. The amount you earned would not change. By the time 40 years rolls around, you will have made around $1,800.

- **Compound interest** enables one to gain more interest on the interest they are earning from an investment. For example, if you have $1,000 and earn 2 percent each year following the initial investment with compounding interest, the outcome is totally different than with simple interest. By the time you hit the end of your first year, you would have $1,020. By year two, you would end up with $20.40 instead of just $20. If you leave it alone for all 40 years, you will then have earned $2,200.00. That's more than $400 than utilizing the process of simple interest.

Creating Savings Over Time

As you can see, if you were to invest $1,000 in an account that only yielded 2 percent, your money would not grow at a very fast rate. The key to investing is constantly contributing money to that investment, which enables you with additional money that earns compound interest. The magical aspect of compound interest is that the more you contribute, the quicker you will see your money grow! Keep in mind that compound interest works better for you if you leave that money alone for a longer period of time. Again, a perfect reason to start early and build over time.

For example, let's say you are 25-years-old and you begin by investing $5,000 in a savings account. If you put $200 in each month during a span of 40 years, your money can grow as much as $158,900.00 by the time you reach the ripe old age of 65. If you contribute $500 each month for 40 years, you will have earned $380,700. But if you manage to start just five years later, you will only end up with $315,9oo+. See how starting early gives you the advantage of earning tens of thousands of more dollars?

Inflation

Another key aspect in the investment world is inflation, which has the potential to damage your potential for return. A good rule to follow when it comes to savings is to figure that inflation will be 3 to 4 percent each year. What this means for you is that you real returns will become eroded if your account fails to have a high yield. It is recommended to look for a savings product that offers higher yields in the first place, such as CDs, online savings account, etc.

Inflation may not be fighting against your yields at this very moment, but in the future, the rate of interest will likely rise. If you contribute more to your savings, you will find that your contributions will grow at a much quicker rate.

You Want to Earn Interest, Not Pay It

Compound interest is a pretty nifty tool, right? Beware, however, for it can function the opposite way as well.

Let's take a credit card company for example. A typical one charges around 20% in interest on unpaid balances each month. If you have an unpaid balance of $1,000, it will turn to $1,200 of debt by the time the year ends. You need to reverse the load of debt you have by applying the principles of compound interest. Transfer credit card debt to an interest plan with lower rates. Or, pick a loan with a yearly interest payment, instead of one with a monthly or quarterly required payment.

There are many investment vessels you can use to build up your compounding as well as maximize your efforts to build wealth:

High-Interest Savings Accounts

These accounts can be hard to come by, but by doing a bit of digging, you can find some awesome rates. If you are wanting to invest now, you should seek out banks that update their interest rates on a regular basis. Just a few percentage points can make a world of difference.

For instance, if you invest $5,000 in an account that grows 0.8 percent of compound interest within a period of 5 years, your return will be $5,200. But the same investment of $5,000 at a rate of 2 percent will yield you $5,500. For that extra $300, it is worth that extra time to locate a better interest rate to invest your money into. Bankaholic is a great start for consumers in the United States, and High-Interest Savings (https://www.highinterestsavings.ca/chart/) is a good choice for Canadian consumers.

Another good thing that brings you peace of mind is that the going rates on bank websites are often negotiable. Before you agree to a set rate, no matter if it is for a car payment, savings account, or load, ask the provider if they have any discretion. You might get an interesting look, but just for asking, the lender may just provide you the best rate available!

Certificate of Deposit (CDs)

CD's are very secure vehicles of investment, for they offer a fixed rate of interest till they hit a specific date of maturity. The advantage of CDs over high-interest savings accounts is that they guarantee that the interest rate will not change during the time you are investing. The catch is, your money is not liquid, which means you have to keep it locked away for a specific period of time. If you go to withdrawal it early than that date, you will have to pay a penalty. What you earn from the interest is also taxable.

There are various kinds of CDs and GICs (Guaranteed Investment Certificates). Each has their own set of terms, as well as pros and cons. As of now, CD and GIC rates of interest are about even with accounts that have high interest rates.

Stock Dividend Payments

Stocks that pay you dividends are a fantastic way to add additional income to your life. To grasp the absolute power of investing in these kinds of payments, read this example of the story of Grace Groner:

Grace was hired as a secretary after she graduated college in 1931. She worked for 40 years in this position. Grace did not earn an amazing salary as a secretary. She bought clothes from thrift stores and personal home sales and lived in a tiny apartment that was given to her after a friend died.

A few years later in 1935, Grace purchased a few shares of the company's stock that she worked for, at $60 per share. Her investment total was $200. Grace did not sell her share. Through the ways of share splits, dividends, and dividend reinvesting, when she passed away in 2010, her portion of the shares was worth over $7 million. By simply starting with $200, Grace was able to take full advantage of the power of compounding for roughly 75 years.

The Answer to Investing

By grasping how to maximize the usage of compounding interest, you too can harbor the power to create a substantial chunk of wealth over time. The vital key to keep in mind is that no matter how good or bad your finances are right now, you can change your financial future thanks to compounding.

CHAPTER 3: THINGS TO KNOW BEFORE YOU INVEST

Many people never take the time to invest because they follow their belief of "my money is not safe within the markets." This is the conclusion many folks have, especially after the devastation the markets faced back in 2008. Stocks were sold, and many watched their 401k's become 201 and even 101k's. But now, those who had little faith in the markets before are started to get their feet wet in the world of investing once again. The stock market has since been doing spectacularly and proving all those skeptical journalists dead wrong.

Are you considering getting back into investing in the market? Well now might be the most perfect time to avoid the errors that many trap investors use to eat away at their gains. This chapter outlines how to invest your hard-earned money wisely with these valuable tips!

Know the Investing Costs

One of the biggest mistakes investors make is paying large amounts to invest their money. Stockbrokers, tax consultants, and financial advisors are not cheap and can easily eat away at any gains you receive within your investment portfolio.

The fees that Wall Street hides from investors is in the tiny print on your quarterly statements. And even if you were to take the time to read them, you would probably have a very hard time even understanding what they say. If you fail to learn what fees you are being charged with, you probably should avoid those services in the first place. Rule of thumb: if the fees are not completely clear and easy to understand, avoid them at all costs.

Here are the biggest sources of costs it takes to invest that you should keep in mind:

- **Inflation** is an ultimate killer of investment portfolios. If your gains of investment fail to keep ahead of inflation, you will lose money because the value of your money gets eroded away.

- When your investment advisor informs you how much you have made, they are more than likely talking about your gains before **taxes**. But the reality is, you never actually take home your pre-tax gains, just the after-tax ones. You must understand how the tax system will take care of your investments. You will also need to keep in mind what future development of the tax codes might be and how they will affect your investments as well.

- Mutual funds and brokers will charge you a fraction of the amount based on how big or small your portfolio is, which are known as **advisory fees.** Often times the number they charge is so small that you do not think much about it, but 2 percent can add up quicker than you think.

- Each time you sell or purchase a stock, a fee is charged by your brokerage, known as **brokerage commissions**. They are typically flat fees based upon either the amount of stock you buy or the trade. The lower, the better is the best way to go here.

Decrease Your Costs

Since you are now aware of the costs that can damage your overall portfolio, you are now in a place where you need to figure out methods of decreasing them. Here are the best things you can do to counteract those fees:

- **Invest in mutual and index funds that cost the lowest.** This obviously seems pretty straightforward, but many investors overlook this simplicity. There are very small fractions of a percent that can make a huge impact on your portfolio over many years.

- **Pay attention to cost changes.** Even though you invested in a low-cost fund, to begin with, does not mean that the costs will stay low. New competitors and products are introduced to the world all the time, which may play a role in increasing your fees.

- **Pay Capital Gains, not Income Taxes.** Active brokerage accounts or investment funds that generate many sales will also create high taxes on gains. You can reduce your tax costs by sticking funds that are passive and can make investments long-term. You will pay lower capital instead of those high-income taxes. Just be aware that some eliminated this benefit to investors.

- **Purchase Inflation Protected Treasuries.** To decrease becoming exposed to the inflation process, you can purchase gold, which has a tendency to go up in value when the value of money decreases. But this is not a practical method for the majority of investors. A simpler method is to put part of your overall portfolio in a TIPS, or a Treasury Inflation Protected Securities. While this will not shield you from collapses in the government, it can protect you from about everything else.

- **Invest in a Retirement Account.** If you are investing to mainly save up for retirement, ensure that you are utilizing an account that is also paired with tax advantages that let you avoid taxes not only now but in the future as well. This advantage can take you far, and the good news is that many big employers offer these accounts.

Gain Exposure to Upside Surprises

As an investor, you will get a first-hand look at how unpredictable the market is. This is a big problem for many investors because you are only allowed to invest for the gains you hope you will have in the future. As an investor, you are also a speculator for uncertainty in future events.

One way to handle all that uncertainty is to create a situation of upside exposure. What this means is that you should be willing to put money down on a number like you do when playing roulette. In other words, do not be stupid and make big bets randomly. Search and locate events that look highly unlikely, something that many others say is unlikely to occur. Make a small investment in that event, just remember that the odds are stacked against you.

For example, buying a $1 lottery ticket is not a good way to expose yourself to the upside of winning. This is because your investment of that dollar is too much for many jackpots in the first place. But if you purchase a lottery ticket with just a few coins of change, that would make more sense. The point here is, making riskier bets is perfectly fine as long as the cost to make them is low.

Diversify

Everyone has learned not to put all your "eggs in one basket." Diversifying your investments is vital. But many do not grasp how challenging it is to really diversify their money. Here are some pointers to get started:

- **Have more than one manager.** Many people think they are diversified because of the assortment of assets they had listed in their portfolios. The sad truth is many investors are exposed to a whole different type of risk, which is getting ripped off by their asset manager. Diversification should happen in every level.

- **Time preference.** Your investment portfolio should have assets in it that you expect to appreciate at different increments of time. This is a heavily overseen aspect of investing. Doing this helps you to avoid having those investments to be keyed in all at once, possibly during a time when the market could very well be crashing.

- **Mix assets.** You are not diversified if you own twenty or even one-hundred stocks and not anything else. You should strive to have a variety of classes when it comes to assets, such as treasuries, gold, bonds, stocks, etc. This makes you *truly* diversified.

Engage in Legal Insider Trading

If you hold a piece of valuable intel about an organization that you know others do not have access to, you should think about trading on that intel. There is nothing illegal about trading information that is secret that took you lots of hard work to come across. This is one of the best and only ways you can ever beat the market.

Here is the catch, however; do not do this if the intel that you withhold about an organization is one that you or a spouse works for. Do not act on this even if you hold an obligation to a third party. You can easily violate SEC rules when trading non-public information from a place of business you work for.

Don't Fall for "Hot Stocks"

Every single year some businesses run features in papers and magazines about hot stocks and sectors that are coming up. Honestly, you should never read these articles and avoid them as much as possible. The only thing these do is cause you distraction.

The same concept is true for investing in advice from people like Mr. Jim Cramer. When markets open the following morning, a stock that Cramer recommended is more than likely way to pricey. If you really want to place money in these hot stocks, wait a couple to a few months. If it goes down and you still think it is a good investment for your money, go for it. But the key here is to avoid that initial rush of wanting to trade by going for the bait of when it is first announced.

Ignore Most of Your Quarterly Statement (But Still Read it!)

Let's be honest, who really *likes* to read their statements in the first place? This is especially true when the market is not ideal. They will make you feel poor, ignorant, and can bring down your overall self-esteem when it comes to investing. But yes, you need to read *your statement*! You should not be reading them for your returns, but rather to keep track of those investing fees. Many brokerages and funds tap on extra fees in hopes that investors will not notice them.

Negotiation is Possible for Just About Anything

If you are signing on to investing in a sizeable fund, expect to pay the required fees. If you plan to create a brokerage account, however, you have a lot more room to negotiate what these fees are.

Financial advisors will say the fees are set at a certain rate and cannot be changed, but do not believe them. There is a plethora of fees offered by brokerages. The thing is, they are not obligated to find the best-priced ones for you. You need to negotiate with your broker to find the lowest fee they can. Once they give you a quote, simply tell them "these are not the fees I am looking for."

Invest in Passive Life Cycle Funds and Reinvest with Dividends

This tip can be a daunting one that takes some work, but welcome to the world of investing! The best thing you can do to set yourself up for success in the realm of investment is to invest your money in a lifecycle fund that is low in cost. These funds can change your allocation of assets as your age.

You should also take the step of reinvesting those dividends in your funds. Each year you should take the time to examine fees and every five years ask for assistance in analyzing your asset allocation. If you get divorced, buy a house, get married, have children, etc., you will want to re-examine these allocations.

You Will Never Be Able to Beat the Market

And you will not want to anyways! Here are crucial things you need to know when it comes to investing:

- Even if you were to learn how to beat the market, you could not beat it. If you try, you will more than likely end up farther behind than when you started.

- That being said, there really is no reason you should want to outsmart the market anyways. The great news here is that you do not have to fight against the market to receive gains from your investments. The real goal of investing is to save money for later in life and not let it lose value. Investing is not about getting rich quickly.

- Sometimes, returns will be a lot worse then you expect them to be. In the future, diversified investment strategies might not pay off as well. Changes in demographics, the spread of information, the age of the average investor, and declining markets have huge impacts. Never count on bonds and stocks to go up along a trend for forever.

CHAPTER 4: INVESTING IN STOCKS

Let me ask you this: Would you rather have $108,000 or $600,000?

The answer for everyone is obviously the same! But how in the world can you as one person make $600,000?!

Well, start with investing $300, then add $300 monthly over the course of 30 years, and you will accumulate $108,000. But here is the difference when it comes to compounding at different interest rates:

- 2 percent = $147,600
- 5 percent = $245,600
- 10 percent = $620,700

The vital lesson to learn here is that saving is important, but what you earn on that saving is crucial to making more money with those investments. Sadly, in today's world, there is no method to earn anything close to that 10 percent when it comes to insured savings accounts. It is even challenging to earn 2 percent at times. The only method to get a higher rate of return is to take a risk and invest in stocks.

What Are Stocks?

Stocks are equity investments that serve as a part of ownership within a business. They entitle you to a part of that corporations earning and assets. Common stocks provide shareholders voting right, but no actual guarantee that they will receive dividend payments. The preferred stocks offer no right to vote but promise those dividend payments.

Shareholders receive a paper certificate of their stock, which is known as a security. This verifies the number of shares they own. But today, ownership is recorded electronically. This means that shares are held by your brokerage firm for safe keeping.

Stock investing can be awfully tricky. When it comes to successfully stock investing, you will need to get into a business mindset. Before you go out and purchase a stock, you should master all of the fundamental parts that make up investing. You will not become an investor overnight, but once you grasp the basics, you only then should be investing in stocks. This way, you have the confidence to make the right decisions.

Depending on how you measure stocks, they have averaged around 8 to 10 percent annually over the past century. Stocks always involve risk, which is why they pay much more than the average saving account. If you avoid risk, you create a whole new risk, which is not having enough money to adequately survive in your years of well-deserved retirement.

Stock knowledge is important! And contrary to popular belief, it is not rocket science.

The Rules of Investing in Stocks

Rule #1: Only Long-Term Money

Stocks would not even exist if they did not pay more than the alternatives that are less risky. The key phrase in this rule to remember is "over time." The longer your investment, the lower the risk when it comes to stocks.

Day trading is strongly risky because no one really knows what is going to occur each day. If you are not one to be extremely risky with their money, aim to invest in quality stocks because they show more value over time historically.

Rule #2: Moderation

Since the stock market is risky, it is vital to never put all your money in one place. If you are 25-years-old, for example, you should subtract your age from 100. This means that 75 percent should be put into stocks and the other 25 percent should be placed in savings.

Rule #3: Utilize Mutual Funds

Many people like purchasing individual stocks, but it is not necessary. You can function perfectly fine with a mutual fund as you lower your risk of reducing hassle at the same time.

Mutual funds are essentially a big pool of investments. It can be both a stock pool, which is a pool of stocks or a bond pool, a pool of bonds. Or, some mutual funds withhold both stocks and bonds, which is called a balanced fund.

Mutual funds allow you to spread the risk of investing in stocks by diversification among many stocks instead of just in a few. They also have people in them that do both the buying and selling and they keep track of the majority of that pesky paperwork for you.

Mutual funds fall into two categories:

- Index funds is similar to owning the entire stock market but is represented with an index. All the index fund managers have to do is buy the stocks, making it simple, and the fees minimal.
- Actively managed funds employ folks that claim they can outperform the indexes in index funds. They demand higher fees for their expertise.

Rule #4: Do Not Time the Market

You will quickly find yourself sitting on the sidelines if you try to time the market, especially when and if it takes off or crashes. There is a simple way to approach the stock market: with dollar cost averaging, which is also referred to as systematic investing. To do this, all you must do is invest in fixed amounts, such as $100 during regular intervals. This method works well because it automatically purchases more shares when they are cheaper, and fewer shares when they are more expensive.

Rule #5: There Are No Rules!

If you do not plan to take a bit of a risk, you will never reap the rewards. The trick to lessen the nightmares of investing is to be wise about it.

No rule states you must invest in stocks. If you dislike stocks, invest elsewhere, such as collectibles, peer-to-peer lending, side businesses, real estate, etc. There are many other avenues to beat the bank. While some involve more time and risk than others, their rewards can have the potential to change your life.

CHAPTER 5: INVESTING IN REAL ESTATE

Purchasing real estate is a lot more than locating a new place to call a home of your own. Investing in real estate has been over time a progressive way to invest hard-earned cash and is a very prevalent investment vehicle.

The real estate market has tons of room to pocket huge gains by purchasing and owning. It is significantly more complicated than just placing investments into stocks and bonds.

Rental Properties

This is a venture that is as aged as the practice of owning land. People will purchase a property and lease it out to an inhabitant. The proprietor, known as the owner of the land, is then in charge of paying the loan, assessments, and expenses of keeping up with the property.

The proprietor charges lease to cover the greater part of the costs. A landowner may charge more since their goal to make a profit. However, the most widely used method is persistence, so they just charge enough lease to cover costs until the home loan has been paid in full, then the lease moves toward becoming a solid investment. The property may have appreciated in value through the time the loan was active, leaving the proprietor with a profitable resource.

There are, obviously, flaws in this seemingly "perfect venture." You can end up with a terrible occupant who destroys the property or you will end up having no inhabitant at all. This then leaves you with a negative income, leaving you to scramble to cover your home loan installments. This is why you should always opt for a territory where opening rates are low and pick a place that individuals will have to lease.

When you purchase a stock, it sits in your fund and over time, creates increments in value. When you invest in rental properties, many obligations come with being a proprietor. If the heater quits working, it's you who gets the telephone call. If you do not mind being a part-time and unpaid handyman, this may not bother you in the slightest. If you have the money and are willing to pay for these issues to be taken off your hands, it is a good investment to hire a property supervisor who would be more than happy to assist.

Real Estate Investment Groups

Real estate investment groups are similar to small shared assets for investment properties. If you wish to own a property to rent out, but do not wish to deal with all the hassles that being a landlord has to offer, a real estate investment group is more than likely a much better option.

An organization will buy or create a group of apartments or condos which then enable speculators to get them through the organization, they then allow them to join this group. A financial specialist can then claim one or various units of living space, but the people working the investment manage all of the units, which include dealing with upkeep, promoting empty units and meeting occupants. In return for this kind of management, the organization takes a percentage of the lease.

There are a few variants of investment groups, yet in a regular form, the rent is in the financial specialist's name and the units get together a bit of all the lease agreements to prepare for infrequent opening, implying that you will get enough to pay the home loan regardless of whether your unit is never actually leased out.

The nature of investment groups depends on the organization that is offering it. It is a protected method to get into real estate investment, yet many are still defenseless against expenses that frequent the mutual fund industry. Once again, performing adequate research is key to success.

Real Estate Trading

This is the intriguing and challenging side of real estate investing. Like investors who are miles away from a purchase, the land brokers are an altogether unique group. Land brokers buy properties with a goal to have them for a brief time, around three to four months. This is when they plan to offer their property purchase for an investment. This procedure is called flipping properties and is focused on purchasing properties that are either underestimated or are in an exceptionally hot market.

Unadulterated property flippers won't put any cash into a house for upgrades; the investment needs to have the incentive to turn a profit without adjustment or they will pass it by. If a property flipper gets captured in a circumstance where he or she can't empty a property, it can be damaging to the financial specialists as it would mean don't keep enough prepared money to pay the home loan on a property. This can prompt misfortunes for a land broker who can't offload the property in a terrible market.

An inferior of property flipper likewise exists. These financial specialists profit by purchasing sensibly evaluated properties and including an incentive by remodeling them. This can be a more drawn out term which relies on upgrades. The restricting part of this journey is that it takes time and just enables financial specialists to go up against one property at any given moment.

REITs

Real estate has been around since practically the dawn of time, where our ancestors who were cave dwellers began to chase out strangers from their space. It is no wonder that Wall Street has figured out how to turn real estate into a trade on an open market.

A real estate investment trust (REIT) is created when a trust, also known as an organization, utilizes a financial specialists' money to purchase and work salary properties. REITs are bought and sold on significant trades, much the same as some other stock. To keep up the status as a REIT, an organization must give out 90% of its benefits as profits. REITs are then abstained from paying corporate income tax, though a standard organization would be saddled by its benefits. After that need to choose if they wish to circulate its after-impose benefits as profits.

Much like standard profit paying stocks, REITs are a strong venture for securities exchange financial specialists that need customary wage. In contrast with the previously mentioned kinds of land speculation, REITs permit speculators into non-private ventures, for example, shopping centers or office structures and are exceedingly fluid. At the end of the day, you won't require a real estate broker to enable you to money out your venture.

Leverage

Except for REITs, putting resources into real estate provides a financial specialist a device that isn't accessible to securities speculators, which is the use of the REIT. If you are looking to buy a stock, you need to pay the entire estimation of the stock at the time your request. Regardless of whether you are purchasing on the boundary, the sum you receive is still substantially less than with real estate.

Many "traditional" home loans require a 25 percent down-payment that is contingent upon where you reside. There is a plethora of types of home loans that require just a tiny 5 percent. This shows that you can control the entirety of the property and its value by paying a small amount of the aggregate esteem. Obviously, the loan will, in the long-term, pay the estimation of the house at the time you purchased it, but you are still in control of the moment the papers are agreed on.

This is an aspect that encourages both the flippers of real estate properties and owners of real estate. They can make a temporary contract on their homes and put up front installments on more than one property. Regardless of whether they lease these out with the goal that inhabitants pay the loan or they sit tight for a chance to receive a greater investment, they are in full control, in spite of having paid for just a piece of the aggregate esteem.

The Bottom Line

We have taken a gander at a few kinds of real estate investing methods. Nonetheless, we have just touched the most superficial layer. Inside these cases, there are endless varieties of ways to invest in real estate. Likewise, with any venture, there are huge amounts of overall potential when it comes to real estate. This does not imply that it is a guaranteed gain. Make watchful decisions and weigh out all of the pros and cons of your activities before taking a dive into the real estate game.

CHAPTER 6: INVESTING IN BONDS

While the word "bonds" sounds awfully boring, it is far from it. They are a safe haven for retired and rich folks that do not wish to lose their money. Bonds play a role in your investment plan for other reasons as well. They help add diversity to your portfolio as they control risk. However, bonds can be a complicated subject to thoroughly grasp.

Bonds are completely different from sticks. Stocks that are well-selected tend to go up over a long period of time but can go down in the short run. Bonds also create a very nice steady stream of income that you can then reinvest or utilize for living expenses later on. Their price has the potential to fluctuate, but the overall bond remains the same. Plus, bonds like municipal ones can produce a tax-free income!

Getting Started with Bonds

It is crucial to understand the concepts of price, interest, maturity, and yield before jumping into making an investment in a bond. Small investors should really stick with high-quality bonds.

- Interest: The majority of bonds pay you interest semiannually.

- Maturity: When a bond reaches its maturity, they then have the power to pay the investor back at face value. Bonds that mature in two years or less are short-term ones, with 10 years being intermediate and 10+ years being long-term bonds. Most bonds are issues with 20 to 30 years maturity.

Types of Bonds

- **Zero-Coupon Bonds:** Many common bonds you receive interest payments every six months. But with zero-coupon ones, they credit you interest. However, it doesn't pay till it totally matures.

- **Uncle Sam's Bonds:** If you like peace of mind, these types of bonds are the essential way to go!

  - **Treasury bills** mature in a year or less with new ones being sold on a weekly basis. The minimum amount to purchase is $1,000. They are exempt from local and state taxes as well.

  - **Treasury bonds** take 10 or more years to mature. The minimum to purchase one of these bonds is $1,000.

- **U.S. Agency Securities:** Are similar to government bonds when it comes to safety, but be aware of the risks they hold as well.

- **Municipal Bonds:** These depend on which bracket you are when it comes to taxes. The higher the tax bracket, the more likely you will receive a better benefit than those that are issued by local and state agencies.

CHAPTER 7: INVESTING IN BUSINESS PARTNERSHIPS

Investing your hard-earned cash into a business is one of the best and most prevalent methods of investing in the journey of financial dependence for those small businesses. It is a great way to grow and create an asset that, when led under proper conditions, provides numerous amounts of cash those other investments cannot compete with. Small businesses grow through the means of representing the most crucial financial resource the family owns, other than their home.

Investments in business are built as either a limited partnership or a limited liability company. The limited liability is by far the most used, for it combines the best attributes of corporation and partnerships. When you are pondering over investing your money into a small business, there are two main types of positions you can choose to take:

Equity Investments

When you make an equity investment in any business, you are essentially purchasing part of the overall ownership, or in other words, taking a piece of the pie. Equity investors give capital with cash in exchange for the percentage of both profits and losses.

The business then can utilize this allotment of money for a variety of things that are business related, from funding expenditures, the running of daily operations, decreasing debts, purchasing other owners, creating liquidity, or hiring new employees. This type of investment when it comes to small businesses results in bigger gains but comes with a bit more risk. If expenses become higher than the amount of sales, the losses get handed over to the investor. If things go well, the return can be exponential.

Debt Investments

When you make a debt investment in a business, you are loaning money in exchange for repayment of your loan down the road, along with income made from interest. Debt capital is given in the form of loads with amortization or the purchasing of bonds that are issued by the business itself.

The biggest advantage to debt investments is that you get a nice cozy spot in the structure of capitalization. This means that if the company fails, the debt takes priority over stockholders, also known as equity investors. The highest level of debt incurred is a first mortgage secured loan that has a lien on a piece of property or an asset that is very valuable, typically the brand name.

Which Type of Partnership Investment is Better?

When it comes to life in general, especially when it comes to the subject of businesses, there is no simple or clean-cut answer. For example, if you were an early investor of McDonald's and purchased equity, you would be very well off. If you had purchased bonds with the debt investment method, you would have earned a decent amount in return, but by no means as spectacular as the other.

Things to Know Before Investing in Partnerships

- **Beware of the opportunity** by asking why the opportunity is available for investing in the first place. Usually, businesses are trying to raise money, which usually means they failed to get a loan from a bank. You need to find out the story behind their reasonings.

- **Understanding the structure** can help you to determine how the legal systems and the IRS view the profits and liabilities of the business you are considering investing in. There are major chances that the business could fall out. You can be responsible for bills that are unpaid or other liabilities depending on the structure of the business.

- **Keep in mind that you may not see returns for years,** so do not assume that investing in a business will equal automatic profit. Startups especially need all the money they can get, with earnings usually being added back into the business. Returns for investors may not be present for 3 to 5 years or more.

- **Have an exit strategy planned** just in case it takes too long for you to see solid revenue from your investment. You do not want to burn through all your investment before a business opens its doors.

- **Do your homework** before investing your money into a startup business. You want to know the background of the business and have a good understanding of it and its competition. You should also request a business plan that includes a description, financial plan, market analysis, etc.

CHAPTER 8: INVESTING IN PRECIOUS METALS

Investing in gold and silver is quite simple, as well as fun and highly profitable. Almost anyone can learn how to begin purchasing gold and silver as a physical way to wealth. Gold and silver, along with other precious metals, have the strength to hold their value, which can mean not only a beautiful but a long-term investment as well.

The process of purchasing, selling, and holding precious metals involves some annoyance that you need to understand to be successful and gain awesome returns.

What Are Precious Metals

Precious metals are naturally occurring, rare, and challenging to find than other metal types. The rarity of these metals gives them high economic value. They are still valued for their use in commodities, jewelry, art, and investments.

- Gold
- Silver
- Palladium
- Platinum

Precious Metal Investing

Precious metals are highly valued in many industries, so they are traded on a regular basis in world commodity markets. People in all countries have some sort of need for precious metals, which means they are constantly changing due to the supply and demand for them.

These metals can be bought by people as investment vehicles. This is done through a mint or a broker, in which it can be purchased in a few formats, such as in its physical form, stocks, mutual funds, ETF funds, etc. Those that choose to buy precious metals in their physical form usually purchase bars, bullion, or coins in various shapes and sizes, depending on the amount they purchased.

Inflation is a common risk when it comes to investing in metals. Buying them at the present time at the current price protects their value against future metal inflation, which is why they make for ideal investment vessels. This is certainly true with gold, the most popular investment metal due to its high value and availability.

Buying Precious Metals

Investing in precious metals is a great method if you are looking to make quick profits and increase your savings for future living. You can purchase or sell small to large amounts of metals on a regular basis to make money daily. You can also buy small to medium allotments to hold as a part of a retirement account.

The best metals to buy are silver and gold because they are the ones most often used as currency. You will need to talk to a stockbroker or a dealer of precious metals to buy them. You also will need to do adequate research on the various methods of precious metal investing to discover all the methods in which you can gain a profit from each precious metal individually and together.

CHAPTER 9: INVESTING STRATEGIES

When it comes to investing, any amount of knowledge adds significant value to you as a growing investor in the market. This chapter is loaded with strategies to help you invest the best you can as a beginner in the world of investing.

Don't Wait, Start Now

There will never be a better time to begin the investing process. Don't wait till you get a higher paying job or save enough money. If you are a procrastinator, this will never come for you. Start now, with a little from each paycheck you receive. The quicker you start, the better you will be and the bigger of an investment you will incur over time as it matures.

Expert Advice

Experts in the investing world can help you to understand all of the investment options that are open to you. You will be able to determine which avenues of investing are right for your lifestyle with the help of an investment planner. Many are free! Open an account and link your accounts.

Start Out Simple

After you are knowledgeable about the options you have, it is recommended to start with the simplest and learn the rest as you gain experience. You can make mistakes and not feel bad about it when you are just starting out, with small investments like $100.

Know Your Goals

Before you make the step to invest, know what your goals are for venturing into investing in the first place. Do you want to start saving for retirement? Do you want to grow a fund for your kid(s) to go to college? Investing is much different from just saving money, it is a long-term process.

Know Your Options for Investment Vehicles

Make sure you plan out what you wish to invest in as well when deciding your goals. You can invest in brokerage accounts, college funds, 401k's, etc. Some of these have big tax breaks that will make them a clear advantage.

Open an Investment Account

Once you have made a clear decision about what vehicle you wish to use and what your goals are, it will be much easier to sign a form and get funds rolling into an account. Make sure you have a reliable platform to buy and sell your investments.

Start in Auto Investing

You should start this as soon as possible with regular contributions. Many brokerage accounts totally support monthly investment options.

Learn a Hands-On Approach

Many people think that once they make an investment, they just let it sit there and it will do the hard work for them. It is vital to track your investments to check to see if they are growing. Make it a priority to check into them every six months to a year.

Picking an Amount to Start Investing

This will be a major decision when it comes to handling your budgets and the increments you will make to your investment over time for it to grow substantially.

Make Investing a Habit

To increase your investment earnings over time, you have to stick to it and contribute regularly. It's kind of like a plant; if you don't water it and provide it with a light source, it will eventually die and not create any produce for you to pick.

Make Baby Steps

Don't expect investments you make to make anything extraordinary any time in the near future. You must learn to be patient and look into other investment options to invest money in as you wait for your others to grow over time.

Be Knowledgeable of Packaged Mutual Funds

This is a great option that many beginners in investing overlook. They are less risky and are quite volatile. The costs for transactions are also low, and every fund is easily managed by portfolio managers who are in charge of rebalancing your portfolio to ensure that proportions are consistent with your investment.

Be Wise When Choosing Stocks

You will never be able to accurately time a stock market, but they are a good option and don't require you to have a lot of capital upfront. If you pick wisely, you will have a peace of mind knowing you will have a stable income.

Take the Time to Learn

It is no secret that there is a lot of information regarding investing. If you are serious about becoming a seasoned investor, go out of your way to purchase investment books, strategize with the investment knowledge you gain. Look online and perform research, checking out companies that peak your interest. Ensure that you are fully aware of what those companies are earning, who their customers are, and more.

Play Safe

Investing is not the time of place to be wild with your money. Make a margin of safety for yourself, but be sure not to be too over-dramatic with your boundaries, as it could keep you from exploring other vehicles of investing or keeping you from taking the risks that are required in investing to reach success.

Don't Impulse Invest

Make sure to always take your time and speak with experts before going out and purchasing stocks, bonds, funds, or another other investment vehicle.

Beat Inflation

No matter what you choose to invest in, try your best to beat the rate of inflation, or you might find that you are losing money rather than gaining it. Simply placing your hard-earned money in a savings account is not a method of investment, but an easy-way-out of doing the hard work to reach your financial goals.

Create an Emergency Fund

Before you go out and start the process of building up your investment empire, make sure to create an emergency fund first. Also, it is a good idea to create an insurance cushion that will protect your money. You never know where the road to investment will lead you.

CONCLUSION

I want to congratulate you for making it to the end of *Investing for Beginners!*

I give you a big pat on the back for reading the entirety of this book, for you are one giant step closer to becoming your very own investor! While money can't buy happiness, it can sure help to build a cushion that brings you peace of mind when life gets a bit rocky. Wouldn't you rather be prepared than sorry?

As you have learned, everyone should learn the basics of investing. Now that you have soaked up all this valuable information, you should feel all that confidence bursting at the seams inside of you. Yes, you can even learn how to invest like the big guys on Wall Street with a bit of basic knowledge, common sense, and a bit of faith in the market.

I hope that everything in this book has given you the information you need to take the next step in investing some of that hard-earned money of yours. All the tools you need to achieve your investment goals can be found in this book as a reference if you get a bit lost.

Good luck my investing friends! Make that money grow!

If you found this book useful in any way, please take a moment from your investing ventures to leave a review on Amazon. It is always appreciated!

DAY TRADING

The beginner's guide to making a fortune from day trading

By Sam Sutton

~~~

INTRODUCTION

Congratulations on downloading your personal copy of *Day Trading*. Thank you for doing so.

The following chapters will discuss some of the many strategies you can use to be a successful day trader.

You will discover how important it is to make sure that you know how each of the strategies works and how they can help you achieve your goals.

The final chapter will explore some of the things that you should not do to be able to day trade successfully.

There are plenty of books on this subject on the market, thanks again for choosing this one! Every effort was made to ensure it is full of as much useful information as possible. Please enjoy!

Congratulations on downloading your personal copy of the *Day Trading*. Thank you for doing so.

CHAPTER 1: PREPARING YOURSELF FOR DAY TRADING

Before you can even think about day trading, you need to make sure that you are fully prepared for the process. Day trading is not a technique or something that you can get involved in quickly, and it should be taken very seriously. It is not a get rich quick technique and something that you need to work at for a long time before you can do the best part of day trading.

There is no way that you can guarantee that you will be successful in day trading, but there are things that you can do to set yourself up for success so that you will not completely fail at the process. Nobody can see into the future when it comes to day trading (or anything, really), but there are things that you can do that will give you a better chance at being able to succeed with your day trading goals.

Try it Out

There is a saying that is nearly as old as time that goes "practice makes perfect." While there is no way to guarantee that you will be good at trading and the chances of being perfect are very low, you should still continue to practice. If you practice all of the time with your day trading, you will be able to learn the techniques that will later translate to you being successful with real day trading.

It is a good idea to try to find somewhere that you can practice. There are many websites that offer day trading practice for free. You won't make any money from the process, but you also will not have to spend any money because you will be able to truly just practice the day trading. There is no money that is involved with it, so you do not have to worry about losing anything. It will give you the chance to truly just practice when you want to learn more about day trading.

When you are practicing, you can get the help from expert day traders. This help can some from true professionals to everyone who does different things within the field of practice. The practice areas are a great place to find someone who can help you with day trading because the people who practice well are the ones who know what they are doing and they are wise for being able to practice the different things that they can do with day trading. It is a good idea to take the advice that they have to offer you. The day trading community is great at helping each other out, and it will allow you to see that there are many different options.

Think Short

Day trading is all about what you can make and sell in a day. There is no day to day work that goes on with day trading, and that is one of the reasons that so many people enjoy the options that day trading has to offer people. When you want to make sure that you are doing different things with your day trading options, you must be able to do it within a day.

Look at the different things that day trading has to offer you right now and then figure out if that will be something that you can sell in the next day. At the close of business of the day that you have purchased your stock, you should make sure that you are going to be able to sell it. This is something that you need to do if you want to be successful at day trading. If you want to make sure that you are doing each of the different aspects of day trading, you need to be always prepared to go back to the day. At the end of each day, you should not have any stocks out or any that you are holding onto – instead, you need to make sure that you sell all of your stocks off at the end of the day.

Not Large

If you have invested in anything else in the past, you may notice that the day trading is much different than that. For example, with the other types of trading, you need to make sure that you are buying the largest and most valuable stock for the lowest amount of money. Day trading is not like that other than you will be spending the least amount of money possible. This means that you should try to find the stocks that are as low as possible and buy them for that reason. They need to be small stocks because you will need to get rid of them at the end of the day.

While you may not be able to make huge profits off of the smaller stocks as you would with larger ones, you will be able to buy more of the smaller ones and have more profits at the end of the day after you have already done what you needed to with the stocks that you are selling off. Just make sure that you get smaller ones so that it will be easier to offload them before the day is over.

You Will Lose

Anyone who goes into the game of *any* type of trading thinking that they are going to win at trades every time that they make one is simply a fool. There is no way to always win with the trading that you have, but you need to make sure that you are trying your best. Just always be prepared to lose because it can be disappointing to think you are going to make a ton of money with every single stock that you have and then have to deal with the problems that come along with not getting the most amount of money possible. You should be sure that you are working to make sure that you are getting the most out of the stock options and that you are going to be able to enjoy everything that the stock process has to offer you whether you are winning or losing.

If you keep your mindset the same and understand that you will lose sometimes, you will be less likely to get disappointed when you do lose money. It can *always* be a downer if you have never lost money on an investment before, but understanding that it *will* happen will ensure that you are not going to have to deal with all of the problems that come along with being down about the process. It can be much easier for you to try to deal with and to move on to be able to continue the investment process if you know that it is going to happen.

CHAPTER 2: AT THE BEGINNING OF TRADING

How you do the first day that you are day trading can make or break your entire career. It can be a great idea for you to get started right away but make sure that you are truly prepared for the rest of the way that day trading works. It is a good idea to try to learn what you can before you get started, but even if you are unable to do that, there are quite a few things that you can do to ensure that you are getting a good start with trading.

Up to Date Trades

There are many ways that you can keep up to date with the stock market and with the different trades. As soon as you think that you are going to start day trading, start watching the market and keeping track of what is going on. By doing this, you will be prepared for the type of market that you are going to come into. Doing this will also give you an idea of what is going to happen with the different options when you get started. You need to make sure that is something that you are prepared for and that you are going to be able to get the most out of when you truly start with day trading.

One way that you can watch the stock market is by watching the news. You should have an understanding of the way that they work, and nearly every news network will publish the information about the stock market that you need to know. You can see whether it is going up or going down and whether you need to be prepared to sell a lot that day or not even get into the market for that particular day.

The other way that you can do this is using the power of the Internet. Most smartphones have applications that allow you to see the stock market. Even if you don't have a smartphone or only have access to a computer, you can use the Internet and watch the stock market. This is one of the easiest ways that you can figure out what you are doing and how much money you can make for that day.

Track Them All

When you are first getting started, you need to make sure that you are keeping track of all of the trades that you do. You need to make sure that you are keeping track of all of your trades, but the ones that you do at the beginning are especially critical. You need to make sure that you know what you are doing and what you are going to do in the future. Writing that information down is easy and will allow you to be able to look back on the record of what you made (including the mistakes that you made).

Some people choose only to write down when they have success, but that is not always the wisest decision. You should keep a log of all of the things that you did right in your day trading career. This can be everything from the way that you need to make sure that you are making money to all of the other options that are included with day trading. Write down when you make a lot of money, write down when you get a trade for a good deal and always write down the profits that you make each time that you make them. You will be able to look back on it and see what you did in the past. This is especially useful for you when you are struggling and want guidance to where you need to go again with your day trading career.

While you may want to write down the results (and the actions that you took to get there) when you do something good, you need to make sure that you are also writing down the mistakes that you made. Mistakes can be hard to own up to so writing them down in a log is one of the best ways to not make the same mistake again. Try to keep the log for the things that went the wrong separate from the things that went right so that there is never a question of whether you should do something again or not. The chances are, if it went south the first time that you did it, it would probably do so again.

Consistency is Key

As soon as you make the decision to day trade, stick to it. This is why you need to make sure that it is something that you truly want to do when you first get started. It can be hard to be able to get to the point that you want and making sure that you make the decision to do it will allow you to truly be successful and get the most amount of money possible. It is always a good idea to stick with decisions that you have made and day trading is no different.

If you need to figure out what you are doing and where you are going to go with the different day trade options, you should make sure that you are getting the most out of the options that are included with the day trading that you have. It can sometimes be hard if you don't know what you are doing, but as long as you follow the steps that are required for getting started, you will be able to make sure that you are doing the most for the different parts of it. There are many different options that are included with day trading.

Being consistent with trading will allow you to make the most amount of money with your trades. Since you are buying and selling each business day, you need to make sure that you are stick to it day after day. There are many different things that go into day trading, and you need to make sure that you are consistent with the day trading options that you have so that you do not have to worry about keeping up with it or missing out on the stocks that could make you a lot of money.

Don't Be Shy

It is not uncommon for beginner day traders to get shy about what they are doing and the options that they have when it comes to trading. This is because they may be worried that they don't know what they are talking about or doing. There are many people who are more experienced than you on the day trading scene but do not let that hinder your ability to trade especially when you are first getting started.

If you see something that you want to buy because you think that it will be a lucrative option, buy it. The chances are that you will be pleased with the purchase that you make and it will make more sense for you to keep trading. If you are nervous about doing it, try it anyway so that you will be able to enjoy the stock without having to worry about any of the problems that come along with it.

This is a principal that goes hand in hand with understanding that you are going to lose sometimes. Take a look at stock, if you want to buy it, just buy it. If you find that you are not going to be able to sell it quickly, you may lose out on the money. That is the worst thing that can happen, though. If you find that you can sell it, you should just make sure that you are getting money from it. The best thing that can happen is that you will get a small profit from it which can allow you to make more money than what you were expecting to make from the stock.

Observe the Trades

Aside from the practice that is going to help you when you are learning about day trading and the different factors that go into it, you should also be observing people who have day trading experience. This means that you need to keep your eye out for professionals and for people who are doing a good job at day trading each time that they do it. Just make sure that you are getting what you can out of the day trading process and that you will be able to learn as much as you can from each of these people.

The people who are professional day traders are usually very open to the trades that they do. Watch them and see what they do. Learn their techniques and build your own off of them. You don't have to trade exactly like they do but learning the right way to do things will give you good options when it comes to your day trading career.

It may be more beneficial for you to make sure that you are trading the right way if you want to watch them first. Try to figure out how they are trading, take that into account and always do your best to provide yourself with the opportunity to do the same as them. Even if you don't have as much money to work with as the longstanding professional day traders, you can still use some of the techniques that they do. You don't even have to buy the same stocks as them as long as you are just making sure that you buy something that is similar and sells it in a way that makes sense for you and the options that you have when it comes to day trading. You can learn a lot from the professionals and model your professionalism off of theirs.

CHAPTER 3: TECHNIQUES TO TRADE WITH

Some people go into day trading blindly and think that they are going to be able to make money from the things that they are doing. This is not the case, and the chances are that you know this. Just because you are reading this book, it is easy to tell that you care about day trading and the different strategies that you can use to be successful. There is a lot more that goes into day trading than just hoping for the best and throwing your money around.

While, like everything with day trading, these things are not going to guarantee that you are going to win each and every time that you want to make a profit, following some of the strategies will help you to have a better time when it comes to making sure that you can truly benefit from day trading. You need to make sure that you can follow, at least, some of the strategies and that you will be able to get more out of them each time that you try different things. You never know what you are going to come across when it comes to day trading so knowing what your strategy will be for each thing that you come across can be helpful to you.

Economics of It

Trading is all about economics. You need to know what is in high supply (and will not cost you a lot) and what is in high demand (and will cost you a lot). If you can buy stocks that are in high supply at the beginning of the day and sell them off at the end of the day because they are in high demand, you will be better able to make sure that you are truly benefitting from the economic factors that come along with trading. It is a good idea always to try and make sure that you are getting the stock for the lowest amount possible and that you are selling it for the highest amount possible. This is the only way that you will be able to make a lot of money.

Knowing that the higher the demand, the higher the price is will help you to have an easier time when it comes to trading. You should make sure that you are only doing things that are in high supply when you first buy them. If you do find something that is in high demand and it is at a good price, snatch it up and then turn right around and sell it for higher. This is the best situation when it comes to day trading and one of the easiest ways that you can make a lot of money at once.

The Reward with the Risk

Similarly to how you need to make sure that you are comparing the demand and the supply of the stocks that you are purchasing, you need to compare the risk of the stock to the reward that you can get from it. This will also help you to decide how you are going to get the stock and how much it is going to work for you.

The risk is what happens when you are buying the stock. This is the amount of money that you can lose on the stock if it does not end up being one that you can win. You should always make sure that the risk is much smaller than the reward that comes along with the stock. This means that the amount of money that you could lose on it is smaller than the amount of money that you could make on it. This doesn't necessarily mean that you are going to lose money or make money on it, but it does mean that you need to be careful about the money that you are spending on different stocks.

On the other end of the spectrum, you should always look at the reward. Do you think that you will be able to sell it for double what you paid for it? While this isn't likely, it is a good way to look at the rewards that are associated with it. If the rewards seem like they are good and like they are something that you will be able to deal with in the long term, you need to take the stock and go with it. Even if you don't get the highest amount possible for the stock when you sell it toward the end of the day, you will be able to make some money from it.

Don't Put Your Eggs in One Basket

Always be careful when you are buying stocks. Even if you find a stock or any investment that seems is, you shouldn't spend all of your money on that one stock. Buy a few of them or even buy more than what you really think is necessary but then stop and move onto a different good stock that will allow you to make even more money. It is important that you do this so that you will be able to be safe with your stocks even if you don't have the right type of investment going on.

By trying out different stocks and making sure that you are investing your money in the right way, you will give yourself a chance to get even more money from the investments that you have made. This means that you need to be sure that you are getting a lot of different stocks that are in different categories and that will allow you the chance to try to do more with the options that you do have. It doesn't always have to be hard for people who are trying to get more out of the day trading options, but it is something that you need to make sure that you are doing the right way.

It can sometimes be hard for you when you are trying to find different stocks. You may not always be able to find exactly what you want, and the expected returns may not be the greatest, but it will be a way for you to make sure that you are going to have something different than one thousand dollars of the same things. If you try to find different stocks that are going to be profitable, you will be able to make money from them. You just have to try.

Different Types of Stocks

There are so many different types of stocks that you can invest in. The different investments will give you a chance to broaden the horizons of your portfolio and will give you a better chance at being able to sell off the ones that you have before the day is over. It can sometimes be complicated to learn all of the aspects of trading so make sure that you are doing it the right way and that you are going to be able to get the most out of it. If you work to make sure that you are getting the right type of stocks, you will have a much easier time when it comes to making money.

You will also be able to sell the stocks more easily. For example, you may struggle to sell 15 of the same stock because that is a big bulk sale. You probably won't struggle, though, selling 15 different stocks that all have different aspects to them. Just make sure that they are all profitable and that they are all going to bring of money that you want to be able to make.

If you can create a profile that is varied and different, you will have a better chance at selling the stocks and getting your money back for them when you are done with the process. It can sometimes be complicated to get the options that you have with selling stocks so make sure that you know what you are doing and that you are going to be able to include everything in the sale of the stocks that you do have. You may even be surprised that some people will want to buy all of the stocks that you have in your portfolio at the end of the day.

The First Hour

Similar to how the first part of your trading is the most important when you start to day trade, the first hour of the day is always going to be the most important part of the trading day. You need to make sure that you get to it early and that you buy your stocks as soon as you can. This is important for two reasons.

The first reason is that you will be one of the first people there and you will have access to the best stocks possible. There are many benefits that come with being the first to get to a specific trading option, but one of the biggest is that you will not have to compete with other people to be able to buy your stocks. You can get the best price possible, and you will have a handle on the day long before anyone else even shows up to buy stocks.

The second reason is that you will then have all day to sell off the stocks that you just bought. You need to make sure that you have as long as possible so that you don't have to worry about getting stuck with them at the end of the day (which is any day trader's worst nightmare). If you buy the stocks at the beginning of the day, you can then take the rest of the day and make sure that you are selling them so that you don't have to worry about having them left over. You will always have a fresh start.

CHAPTER 4:
HANDLING YOUR MONEY

Even people who are really good at managing their money and sticking to a budget may struggle when it comes time to be able to manage the different aspects of the trading process. This, when it comes to day trading. You need to try different things that will help you to save your money, and that will prevent you from spending too much money while you are trading the different amounts of money that you have. It is important that you work to make sure that you can use each of these things to make your trading experience more enjoyable.

The different monetary contingencies that you can put into place are all different and are all intended to be able to help you save money while you are making money. You can choose to use one of them or use them all, but they will help you while you are working on becoming a day trader. Just make sure that you know what you are doing and that you are using them in the proper way. Many of these contingencies are created for people who choose to automatically trade the different things that they have while they are buying and selling stocks during the course of a day.

Limiting Trades

There are some things that you will need to limit to be able to get the most out of the day trading process. For example, you may need to limit the number of times that you trade a certain stock, the amount of money that you put into one stock or the way that you can trade different things. By putting limits on everything that you have, you will be able to ensure that you are going to get the most out of the process and that you are going to be able to enjoy the benefits that come along with trading while you are still managing to save a lot of money on the different processes and on the different price points that you have in different areas.

You can choose to make your decision based on a single trade – for example, you can limit the number of times that you have put the one trade up or you can choose to do it with multiple ones. There are many different combinations that you can make with the trading process, and it is important that you include everything that you need with each of the different options that you choose to put on your limits. Each limit may have a different approach.

When you are setting up the limits that you have on things, you will need to either decide that you are going to do it manually or automatically. Manually will require you to review the process on a daily basis to make sure that you are not going too far above your limits. With the automatic limit setting, you will have limits that will be set ahead of time and will apply to all of the different trades that you do on a daily basis. The choice is yours and will depend on the way that you do things.

Budgeting

Creating a budget for your stocks and your day trading options is nearly the same as creating a budget in any other aspect of life. You need to decide how much you can afford to spend and what you are going to make. With day trading, you also need to figure out how much you are going to put into the trades on a daily basis. This is the limit that you want to be able to stick to each time that you do different trades and on a daily basis. It is important that you work to make sure that you are creating a budget that is completely reasonable for what you want to spend and what you could make throughout the day. You should be sure that you are going to get the most out of it by setting a budget that is reasonable for you.

As long as you are modest with your budget and you plan for any incidentals that could go on with your trades, you should have no problems sticking to the budget. It can be hard to be able to stick to the budget in your personal life, but it should be easy to do it when you are trading different things. As long as you know the amount that you want to spend on a specific day, you should always have a good idea of what that is going to mean for your business and your different trading options. Doing this will allow you to enjoy all of the benefits of trading without having to deal with the problems that come with reckless spending on investments.

Targeting for Price

You should always have an idea of how much each of the investments that are present in your portfolio should cost. This will help you with buying as well as selling and will give you all of the help that you need when it comes to the different options that are included in your portfolio. It is important to make sure that you are going to be able to make money back. If you don't know what something is going to cost you, you may struggle to figure out how much money you are going to get back for it.

Set a target for the price of a stock that you are going to buy. To do this, you must learn how much you want to be able to buy it for. Find out the value of the stock, the amount that you can get for it later on when you do decide to sell it and the average amount that it is going for. Stay within that target price. No matter what happens with your pricing options, make sure that you try to stick to the target price that you originally set. It may be hard to be able to get everything that you need out of it but knowing what your target price is should be enough to help you.

It is also a good idea to set a target price when you are selling your stocks. By knowing the value (and tracking it), you will be able to know what you want to get for it. If you try to sell it at any point throughout the day and you aren't going to be able to get the most amount of money for it, simply try later on in the day. Just be sure that you are not waiting too long to be able to get the money from it because you may end up missing out on the sale that you can get from the stock and you could end up with having the stock stuck in your portfolio at the end of the day so that you are unable to start the day with a clean slate like you are supposed to while you are day trading.

Stop Losses

If you have a stock that is eating up too much money or that is pulling out money from the amount that you want to be able to get, you can always put a stop loss on it. This means that it automatically gets cut off after you have lost a certain amount of money on the stock and that you don't have to worry about it draining anymore of the money that you have in your account. A stop loss is useful for people who use automatic stock options and who want to make sure that they are going to be protected if something would happen that their money is being drained by stock.

A stop loss is a great contingency to have in place if you are planning on doing automatic trading. This is not always the case for people who are new, so it is not something that you will probably need when you are first getting started but just be sure that you know that it is available. Once you start to use auto trading, you should always have a stop loss in place to cut off once you have reached a certain amount that is being taken for the stocks that you wanted to buy originally.

Available for Loss

Everyone sometimes loses when it comes to trading. The real question comes in how much you can lose and what you can do to get the loss out of the way of your trading. The loss is something that you need to be careful with but is also something that you will want to deal with as it comes. It can be helpful to set an "available for loss" balance that you are comfortable with losing.

By knowing the amount that you are comfortable with losing, it will make losses less of a shock to you and can make it easier for you to want to be able to continue trading even after you have started to lose money on the trade. There are many different options that you can set for your loss balance but usually keeping a set amount of money in your balance available to trade is the easiest way to do that.

Always protect your money when you are trading. The point of trading is to make money, and if you are unable to do that, you may not be able to get the most out of the trading process. You should have a good idea of what you have, what you want to be able to have in the future and every other aspect of trading. There are many different options that people who are trading may have to select and to make the right choice is always going to benefit you. It is good to make money, but it is even better to make sure that you are protecting the money that you already have. Losing is difficult, but it can be hard to rebuild money that you had in the beginning.

CHAPTER 5: BECOMING AN ESTABLISHED DAY TRADER

After you have learned all of the steps to go through getting started with day trading and the different processes that are associated with it, you should be able to easily become an established day trader. This doesn't necessarily mean that you will be as good as the people who have been doing it for years, but it does mean that you will be able to work toward making a career out of it. It is not uncommon for people who are working in the day trading field to completely replace their full-time income and to become someone who works for themselves and makes a fortune while doing so.

Financial freedom and stability are both possible once you have established yourself as a day trader and once you have made the decision to stick to it in a way that allows you to be as successful as possible. There are many different options that come along with day trading and making money is nearly always the result of following the right path toward success with day trading.

If you follow these ideas, you will be able to gain financial freedom as a day trader and become among the best people who trade.

Adapt to Flourish

There will be times when you must adapt while you are day trading. There may be things that you are not accustomed to, and there may even be things that you have never seen before. Be prepared for this and make sure that you can handle it. If you are prepared to adapt to everything that is going on with your day trading, you will know the right way to handle it and everything that needs to come along with day trading. There are many different options, and if you don't know the right way to do it, you may find that you are failing as a day trader. That is something you will not want after you have already established yourself as a trader.

Some things that can happen is that there may be unexpected huge fluctuations in prices, there may be problems with the system, and you may lose out on some of the stocks that you wanted. Don't let any of these things get in your way and don't let them bring you down. Just be prepared for them, and there will be no way that they can disrupt your day trading strategies.

If you are able to adapt, you will be great at day trading. You should make sure that you are always prepared for different things and that you don't have to worry about the problems that come along with trading. Day trading is all about being prepared to jump when you need to and that is one of the biggest problems that traditional investors have when it comes to day trading. They are used to having the chance to be able to take their time and figure out what they are doing.

Wait for It

Patience is huge when it comes to day trading. You may find that you have three or four days where you are not able to buy any quality stocks or make any investment. This is something that can be expected and something that you must be prepared for when you are day trading. The positive part of that is that when you have waited for a period to be able to get the trades that you want, you will be able to benefit from the trades that are much better than the ones that you passed up.

Having patience is important in any trading but is especially important in day trading. If you do not have patience and simply buy whatever stocks you want even if you think that they are not going to do well, you may end up with stocks that you cannot get rid of at the end of the day. The point of day trading is to start the next day with no stocks and nothing going on so that you can get a clean slate each time that you start your day.

Waiting for the right opportunity is a way for you to be able to get more out of day trading. It is something that you must be prepared to do and something that can be hard for some people – especially those who are used to not having to wait for anything. You need to make sure that you are trying y our hardest and that you are going to be able to enjoy the benefits that come along with day trading. If you don't have patience, you won't be able to enjoy any of the about because you will never be able to make a truly good deal.

Use Self Discipline

Having discipline can sometimes be hard when you are trying to make money. You may be tempted by the great stocks that you find even if you think that they are not a good price. This is something that can be detrimental to your career in day trading though because if you spend too much money on stocks and then lose all of that money, you won't have the chance to be able to invest more money and be able to make that money.

If you are disciplined with the money that you have, you will be able to save more of it. This means that you can put more money back to be able to invest in higher quality stocks and other investments. It also means that you will be safer if something happens to your trading and the money that you have. Just always be sure that you are going to be able to save money and that the discipline that you are doing is not something that is going to be detrimental.

By not having too much self-discipline, you are going to allow yourself to have the best chance possible. When you are day trading, it can be easy to get caught up and save too much money. This just means that you are keeping too much of it to yourself and not making the investments that you should be to be able to make a lot of money.

There is a delicate balance that lies between being self-disciplined and having too much self-discipline. Try to find that balance, keep it in your sights and always practice it so that you will be able to truly enjoy the process of day trading. It is not fun and there is no point in doing it if you are never able to make any actual money from it.

Past Experiences as Lessons

It is always a good idea to track your trades when you are first getting started, but it can also be beneficial when you are an experienced day trader, too. When you are able to make sure that you are working as a trader, you will benefit from understanding everything that you need to be able to get the most out of your trades. You can use these experiences that you had in the beginning as lessons later on in your trading career. It may seem like it is impossible for you to be able to get the most out of trading if you don't have anything to help you remember but it is a good idea to try to remember this information.

Keeping a log will help you remember what you did in the past that worked and what you did in the past that did not work. Understanding each of these things can make it easier for you later on. If you can keep track of what you spent, how much you invested and all of the options that were included with your spending on different things, you will have a better chance at working toward your goals.

The biggest aspect of trading is learning from your past experiencing. Figure out what worked for you, what didn't and what you can do in the future to make things even better for yourself. There are so many different options when it comes to trading so be sure that you keep track of these and of the options that are included. Write them down and keep them close so that you will always be able to reference them while you are trading.

Pocket that Cash

While you are trading, you should invest some of the profits that you make back into trading. This is the only way that you will grow in your business, and you will be able to improve your business in this way. If you are going to continue to do that, set aside a certain amount of profit to be able to invest back into trading. This is the easiest way for you to figure out how much you need to spend and how much you can afford to put back into your pocket.

It may take some time but you will eventually be profiting above the set amount that you wanted to be able to put back into the business. You should work hard to be able to include all of the different options that are with your trading business and to be able to get the most out of the trading experience. Try to pocket as much as you can after you have put it back. This can go toward your income.

The more that your pocket, the easier it will be for you to replace a full-time job with day trading. You will eventually get so good at day trading that you won't have to worry about working. This will be your income. You may even find that you are making more as a day trader and that you don't have to worry with everything that comes along with having a "real" job. Pocketing your money as much as possible is the first step to building your fortune with day trading and giving yourself the financial freedom to live life the way that you want to.

CHAPTER 6: THINGS YOU SHOULD NOT DO WHILE DAY TRADING

Now that you know all of the things that you should do while you are day trading, you need to take a look at some of the things that you should be avoiding while you are day trading. Doing any of these things can hinder your ability to make money while you are trading and can cause major problems for you if you try to do them. They will not always destroy your day trading business but they have the potential to do so if you are not able to avoid them. Since it can be detrimental to your business, you should always try your best to stop these things before you even have a chance to start them.

Focus on One Strategy

Strategies are great and you absolutely need to have one if you are going to be trading but not having more than a single strategy can be detrimental in the event that you are not able to use that strategy. You should always make sure that you are working your hardest to build up many different strategies and that you are going to be able to do more with what you have. It can be hard to find more than one strategy that works for you and your business but if you are able to find one then you will be able to find more than one.

By allowing yourself to try different methods of trading, you will have more of an opportunity at getting the results that you want. This means that you need to make sure that you are learning as much as possible and that you are going to be able to try different things out. It can be complicated if you do not know what you are doing, but the easiest way to get started with methods of trading is to simply have a backup plan that you can use if your original trading plan does not go the way that you want. The backup plan with is your first alternative.

From there, you can learn even more methods of day trading. Fast selling, wait and watch approaches and trial and error are all a few different ways that you can make sure that you are getting the best experience possible when it comes to the various methods of trading.

Sit Back

Do not ever take a passive approach to trading. You should always be aggressive about your trades, make sure that you are doing everything that you can to be able to get the results that you want and always go after every single one of the trades that you are hoping for. It is a good idea to try different things to get there but don't sit back and wait for those to come to you. It will not only be detrimental to your efforts when it comes to trading but it can also be detrimental in that there are many different options that you can be missing out on.

If you are passive about the trading process, you will miss out on trades. There are no other traders who are successful and took a passive approach. It simply will not happen. Even when you are first getting started, it is important that you try to be as aggressive as possible so that you can get the results that you want. It makes more sense to push to get what you want than to sit and wait for it to just come to you. Trades don't work like that, and there is no magical way for you to get all of the stocks that you want – you have to put in the work and, sometimes, fight to be able to get them.

Do Too Much Effort

There is no reason that you should ever put more than a few hours on getting a stock. As a day trader, that is probably around 10% of your total day that you have available to trade. You don't want to waste it just chasing one thing and there are many different reasons that you may not want to continue chasing that one trade. One of the biggest reasons is that there is no guarantee that you are going to get a lot of money from it or that it will be profitable at all. There are too many other stocks that are available to you for you to waste all of your time on just one of them. It is important that you work toward getting different ones.

If you find that you have wasted too much time on one stock or one investment, you will not be able to get that time back, but you can try to make up for it by working twice as quickly at the other trading options.

This means that you will sometimes need to double down your speed and not waste any time at all on the various trades. It also means that you can sometimes invest in trades that are going to be really bad for your overall profit. It is often just easier to chalk it up to a bad day and move on until the next day. If you can sell the stock that you wasted too much time on, that is beneficial and will allow you to, at least, recoup some of the money even if you can't get the time back.

Rely on Others

Nobody is going to hold your hand when it comes to trading. You need to make sure that you are working for yourself and that you are learning everything that you can on your own. While it is great to have the ability to learn from people who have come before you, they are not going to be the ones who show you what they can do. You need to learn the right way to do it all yourself and to get the most out of the experience of day trading. There are many different ways that you can teach yourself.

Don't rely on others. Rely only on yourself to make sure that you are going to be able to be the best at day trading. Reading this book is one of the easiest ways that you can start out your independent day trading career. Just reading this book is going to give you a great start and will allow you to see that you are truly going to be a great day trader. There are so many options from here that you can take your day trading career to the next level. It is important that you learn the right way to do it.

Stop Trading Out of Fear

If you don't take chances in trading, you will truly struggle to get to where you want to be. You need to take chances at not be afraid to trade something even if it seems like it is going to be a big risk. By allowing yourself the chance to see that good thing can come out of risky trades, you will be getting the upper hand when it comes to your day trading experience. There are many different options that you can enjoy but you will miss out on all of them if you are afraid to take a chance.

For this reason, it is important to weigh the benefits and the risks of trading. You need to figure out what is going to work for you and what is not going to work for you. If it seems like the trade that you are going to be making is going to be a huge risk, you may want to reconsider it. Always weigh the pros and the cons of a trade but also try to do some things that will scare you.

All in all, trading is a risk. You need to decide which smaller risks are things that you want to do and if they are worth it for your personal day trading career.

CONCLUSION

Thank for making it through to the end of the *Day Trading* book. Let's hope it was informative and able to provide you with all of the tools you need to achieve your goals of

The next step is to explore all of the practice options for day trading and put your dreams into actions. You will soon be making a fortune day trading.

Finally, if you found this book useful in any way, a review on Amazon is always appreciated!

www.ingramcontent.com/pod-product-compliance
Lightning Source LLC
Chambersburg PA
CBHW070159230526
45471CB00002B/734